THE DELL WAR SERIES

The Dell War Series takes you onto the battlefield, into the jungles and beneath the oceans with unforgettable stories that offer a new look at the terrors and triumphs of America's war experience. Many of these books are eyewitness accounts of the duty-bound fighting man. From the intrepid foot soldiers, sailors, pilots, and commanders, to the elite warriors of the Special Forces, here are stories of men who fight because their lives depend on it.

☆ ☆ ☆ ☆ ☆ ☆ ☆

IN-COUNTRY!

We were passing a jungle-choked hillside and my fears came true almost immediately. I heard a pop and a hissing sound, followed quickly by another. Gas! There were some noises right next to me on the hillside, and I yanked two high-explosive grenades off my webbing and pulled the pins.

I yelled, "Gas! Don't breathe!" The whole patrol took off and several of the Yards opened fire on the hillside.

"Dei chui!" I yelled. "Don't run! We'll get ambushed!" Everyone by then had a lungful of CS gas, and they panicked, taking off at a dead run.

I flipped my selector switch to auto and opened fire. . . .

Also by Don Bendell

The B-52 Overture

VALLEY OF TEARS *

Assault into Plei Trap

DON BENDELL

A DELL BOOK

Published by
Dell Publishing
a division of
Bantam Doubleday Dell Publishing Group, Inc.
666 Fifth Avenue
New York, New York 10103

ISBN: 0-440-21139-5

Printed in the United States of America

Published simultaneously in Canada

March 1993

10 9 8 7 6 5 4 3 2 1

RAD

DEDICATION

*This book is dedicated
to my old friend Muhammad Ali. You and I
both took opposite paths back then, but we both
did what we believed in, and we each did it full-
out. Our approaches are different, but each of
us prays that someday words like "oppression"
and "war" will be regarded as historical terms.*

—DON BENDELL

VALLEY OF TEARS

Like L.A. freeway, crowded skies,
The Hueys flew us in,
And each man filled with "whats" and "whys,"
That enemy within.

The Plei Trap Valley, filled with hate,
And warriors, blood, and fears.
Hard lessons taught, we fought, and thought,
In jungle wet with tears.

We caught old Charley's Russian truck.
At night, we hid from tanks.
On bent knee, then we prayed for luck
And threw in lots of "thanks."

The VC poisoned jungle streams
And burned my lungs with gas.
We fought the bastards in our dreams
And knew that we'd kick ass.

We fought with cuffs upon our wrists.
And shackles on our legs,
While generals slammed their maps with fists,
And scrambled plans like eggs.

While they were "lifers," we were "pros."
The difference was our pride.
With grease pens they fought paper foes
While warriors fought and died.

That Plei Trap Valley, filled with tears . . .
POWs lost.
While generals laughed and drank their beers,
Our allies double-crossed.

—DON BENDELL

1

Roses and Thorns

Second Lt. Mark Jones had already earned two rock-ers before he started infantry OCS, so he watched with interest the tall, thin soldier who was acting squad leader. High-explosive 105-millimeter howitzer rounds streaked in overhead and pounded the top of the hill, but the former NCO paid them no heed. He was too busy watching the show. So far, the entire company was bogged down because of weak leadership, and Lieutenant Jones watched for potential leaders to assume command positions. The objective above had to be assaulted and, so far, more troops were lying on their bellies firing wildly toward the hilltop than charging ahead. They had to breach the barbed wire and line of bunkers and foxholes.

Smoke swirled lazily in the hot sun, and the acrid smell of gunpowder violated every soldier's sense of smell. Explosions boomed forward of the assaulting troops, and the faint booms of artillery pieces could barely be discerned from their rear.

The lean, lanky squad leader pointed at the barbed wire and yelled at two men, each carrying a long metal tube, "Get the fuck up there with those Bangalore torpedoes! Set one through there, and that one there!" he yelled, pointing at two spots in the barbed wire.

He glanced sideways at Lieutenant Jones and thought, I'm in trouble. Fuck it, he thought, I have a mission to accomplish. Jones just grinned to himself, the facial gesture hidden from his charges.

The squad leader ran back and forth and yelled above the firing, "Everybody on Fire Team Alpha get up off your bellies! Get up! When the Bangalores open the barbed wire, you guys go through! Lay down in line inside the perimeter and set up supporting fire for Bravo Team! Bravo Team, you'll lay down supporting fire for Alpha when the torpedoes blow! Fire and maneuver! Fire and maneuver!"

The squad leader ran back and forth behind the teams and got each member of Alpha Team on their knees. The fuses were set on the Bangalore torpedoes, high-explosive tubes used to blow pathways through barbed-wire barriers. One man on Alpha Team hugged the ground; the rest crouched, ready to go after the explosion. Jones stayed back and observed with interest.

The squad leader ran over to the balker, yelling, "Get up! Get the fuck up!"

The man turned, eyes open wide, and yelled, "They're going to blow! They're going to—"

Face red with fury, the squad leader reached out and yanked on the man's lapels, jerking him to his knees.

He glared into the man's eyes and yelled, "Don't ever argue with me in combat, motherfucker! Now move!"

With that, the squad leader shoved the man forward, just as the Bangalore torpedoes blew up, close but safely, several yards up the hill. The man tried to turn, but the squad leader, ignoring the blinding cloud from the explosions, literally grabbed him by the back of his collar and shoved him toward the hole through the triple-strand concertina wire.

There was no chance for argument. The squawker

ended up as the first man through the barbed wire, followed by the rest of Alpha Team, while Bravo Team, in prone positions, lay down a heavy volume of covering fire. Inside the enemy perimeter, Alpha Team spread out and started firing at the enemy positions themselves while the squad leader ran from man to man behind the Bravo Team members and sent each scurrying, and firing on the run, through the barbed-wire breach. He fired his M-16 and led the team even higher up the hill, positioning them behind trees and bushes, where they lay down cover fire for the first team to move up again.

The squad leader spun around as he was grabbed by the upper arm.

He looked into the serious face of Lieutenant Jones, who said loudly, "Come with me!"

"Yes, sir!"

The squad leader yelled at the Alpha Team leader, "You're in charge! Take over!"

The squad leader followed the lieutenant as he traversed the hill to the platoon leader's position. The two men stopped, and the platoon leader ran to Lieutenant Jones, knowing that it wasn't a midbattle social visit.

Jones said, "You have a pillbox right there on that ridgeline that is spitting out heavy fire. Your platoon's pinned down, man. Now what are you going to do?"

The platoon leader stared at Jones as the wheels turned in his head.

He stumbled on his words as he said, "I guess . . . I . . . a . . . we'll assault on line."

Grim-faced, Lieutenant Jones interrupted and yelled above the explosions and withering fire, "You've done a shitty job! You're fired!"

The lieutenant turned to the squad leader and said,

"Bendell, you are acting platoon leader! Take that machine gun bunker up there!"

Relieved and excited, I grinned and yelled above the gunfire and explosions, "Yes, sir!"

I ran to the nearest squad leader and yelled, "Get me two M-Seventy-two LAWs ASAP."

While speaking, I fumbled with a dark blue oversleeve patch and slipped it on my left bicep. It bore insignia showing I was an acting second lieutenant platoon leader.

The squad leader saw the insignia and yelled, "Yes, sir!"

Spinning, the squad leader ran to several of his men and grabbed portable bazooka-type rocket launchers from them and delivered them to me. I opened one and slipped the other over my shoulders, by the sling.

Jones ran to me and said, "Bendell, what the hell are you doing?"

"Setting an example, sir! It's what they need right now!"

He just stared as I spun and signaled the squad leader in front of me to come back, and hand-signaled the two to left and right to lay down heavy fire and cover me.

Tossing my M-16 to the squad leader, I yelled, "Take care of that for me and cover me!"

Before he could speak, I flashed past him toward the ridge above, still being pounded by artillery fire. Crouched down, my hands helping me run, I climbed in a lung-burning scramble up the slope toward the enemy machine gun. I just knew that I had to do this to motivate the men, whose eyes were all on me. Few of them, myself included, had ever had real bullets and artillery flying around our heads.

The men of the platoon, motivated by seeing their

gung-ho new platoon leader, now lay down a very heavy volume of fire, and were further spurred on by their enthusiastic yells and growls. With them providing good covering fire, I moved forward and across the hillside until I got into position behind a large uprooted stump.

I pulled the safety clip on the first LAW rocket, slid the tube out, and the little plastic see-through sight popped up. Popping up over the top of the root, I quickly sighted and squeezed the first rocket off. There was a tremendous explosion. I couldn't wait: Before the smoke cleared away, I yanked the other tube out, aimed quickly, and fired. The bunker exploded with a loud *whump* and collapsed, great dust clouds billowing out of the wedge-shaped firing port in front and the door in back.

Remembering the slogan for the U.S. Infantry School and being a bit melodramatic, one of my tendencies, I stood, raised my right arm, looked back at the platoon, and yelled, "Follow me!"

With the now-turned-on platoon following me, it was easy to be brave. I streaked up the hill toward the enemy objective. The squad leader, holding my M-16, caught up and tossed it to me as we all charged up the hill. The heat and humidity were like the inside of Satan's wok, and each man in the platoon felt like he was carrying twenty extra pounds, just from the sweat-soaked fatigue uniforms.

Nothing could stand in the way of those screaming young warriors, and we swept over the top of the objective like so many red ants swarming over a dropped crumb of jelly toast. My job wasn't done, though, as I ran from squad leader to squad leader, assigning each squad a sector. Within minutes, the platoon had a spread-out, albeit effective perimeter set up all the way around the military crest of the hill.

The military crest of a hill is an invisible line that runs below the true crest and on which soldiers can stand without being highlighted by the background of the sky. A competent commander never allows anything other than phony bunkers and foxholes to be constructed on the true crest of the hill, where enemy artillery, rockets, and mortars can easily target in.

Lieutenant Jones made it to the top of the hill and kept his eyes on me while I picked up the handset to the AN/PRC-25 radio, more popularly known as the Prick-25. Jones listened while I informed the acting company commander that we had taken the objective and formed a perimeter around the top of the hill. I told him my platoon would hold the objective at all costs until the rest of the company made it there to form a more secure perimeter.

Jones took this all in and went straightaway to talk with Captain Douglas as soon as he appeared with the second platoon to reach the perimeter. The acting CO traveled with that platoon; then I was summoned over to the moving CP. The acting CO got flustered as Jones and another lieutenant, Bob Tarr, hammered at the young man, asking him why my platoon overran the objective without the help of the other two platoons, with the fourth remaining in reserve as a weapons platoon. The man couldn't provide an answer.

"You're fired!" Jones yelled above the noise of the continuing gunfire. "Bendell, you are acting company commander! Take charge!"

Nervous and excited, I said, "Yes, sir!"

I couldn't even think, but just had to act, so I spun and signaled the first squad leader, who had carried my M-16, and yelled, "I've been made acting CO! Can I count on you to accomplish the mission if you take over the platoon?"

The squad leader stuck his chest out proudly and said, "Yes, sir!"

I replied, "Fine! As soon as we get the other platoon on top, you'll take the perimeter from there over to that big dead oak on the other side. You'll have enough men to put out one OP and select a site sixty meters out for an LP for tonight! Put them on the long ridgeline and have your men start digging in."

"Yes, sir," the new platoon leader said, turning to run back to his men, but stopped at the sound of Lieutenant Jones.

"Excuse the hell out of me, Bendell," Lieutenant Jones said, "but who gave you the right to appoint that man platoon leader? That's my job."

I had to be decisive and said, "Sir, excuse me, but I don't have time to argue in the middle of a fucking firefight! You told me to command; I made a decision. If you don't like it, relieve me, but I have a lot to get done quickly!"

We stared at each other for several seconds while Captain Douglas, Lieutenant Tarr, and my eager appointee looked on. Mark Jones, the former tough old SFC who wore his gold bar well, broke into a broad grin.

Jones said, "Hurry up, Bendell! You have a mission to accomplish!"

I grinned, turned, and started barking orders into the company command radio while pushing the RTO swiftly across the hilltop. Within minutes the company perimeter was set up and men dug in, while a number of patrols went out from each platoon to establish observation posts and listening posts, as well as ambush sites on likely avenues of enemy approach. Still other soldiers, having dug their fox-holes and supplementary holes farther back, started clearing fields of fire outside the perimeter immediately in front of their respective positions.

It was a very hot, muggy afternoon, and two men crawled along the hallway floor, folded white Birdseye diapers in their right hands; they dipped them into cans of Butcher's Red Wax, held in their left hands, and rubbed the wax onto the highly polished tile with fast, circular movements. Dressed in shower thongs, fatigue trousers, and white T-shirts, names stenciled neatly six inches below the collarline, each man whistled while they vigorously rubbed the floor, which already had a coat of wax that actually gave the floor the appearance of being covered with a three-foot-thick sheet of clear plastic.

A figure appeared far down the hallway, and one of the floor scrubbers noticed the movement out of the corner of his eye. He turned his head and spotted Lt. Mark Jones headed toward them. The young man dropped his diaper and can in place and jumped up, slamming his back against the brick wall.

"Junior candidates make way!" he screamed at the top of his lungs.

The other man slammed against the wall as well, along with another man who, moments before, had walked out of his room, spit-shining a pair of Cochran jumpboots with double soles and heels. The three men stood at rigid attention, waiting to be pounced upon.

They were relieved when they heard Lieutenant Jones holler, "Carry on!"

He disappeared into his office, and the three men resumed their Sunday afternoon "relaxation activities." It was the one day of the week when the overworked, overtired, overstressed infantry officer candidates could get anything close to relaxation. The rest of the week was filled with spit-shining floors, spit-shining boots, low-crawling through Raider Creek, running back and forth to classes at the Infantry School at Fort Benning, Georgia, and doing so many push-ups that some men worried about literally turning into praying mantises, spending the rest of their life in the "front-leaning rest" position.

I sat on my bunk cleaning the inside of a belt buckle with Brasso and Q-Tips. I had spent hours on my belt buckles in the past, only to have Lieutenant Jones point out the caked white dry Brasso inside the buckle.

"Look at that penicillin, Bendell!" he would shout. "You call that clean? Get over there under the lawn sprinklers and low-crawl back and forth across the grass until my arms get tired."

I'd scream, "Sir! Candidate Bendell, yes, sir!"

Then I would dash across the company formation and hit the ground at the lawn's edge, crawling on my knees, toes, and elbows through the soaking wet grass of 56th Company headquarters, ruining in just seconds my spit-shined Cochrans, shiny black helmet liner, belt buckles, and collar brass, and the triple-starched fatigue uniform, with all the threads carefully burned off the edge of the patches, and the name and U.S. Army tags carefully highlighted with a black Bic pen. I put everything I had into the low crawling, as I knew I would have to dash back into the building, completely change clothes, and rejoin the formation before they departed for the first morning class at the mile-off Infantry School.

The harder I tried, the sooner I'd get "let off the hook" by my tac officer, 2d Lt. Mark Jones. Tactical officers in OCS made an Army or Marine drill instructor, or drill sergeant, look like a Barbie doll.

Across the room from me, my roommate, Karl E.K.E.

Strandberg, an accountant before getting drafted, spit-shined his second extra pair of Cochrans and politely laughed at one of my jokes, which I'm sure he had already heard thrice before. Strandberg, who was well on his way to becoming a qualified infantry officer, liked me but was driven into a frenzy sometimes by my lack of maturity in those days. Karl went into rages most often over the "exorbitant amount" of shaving cream I "wasted" when shaving. I just laughed and never took it seriously, knowing I was simply the brunt of the bookkeeper's frustration from the extreme pressures placed on all the candidates.

Buck Lightell leaned into the doorway from the rubber runner unrolled down the middle of the hallway to protect the shine. Short and stocky, Lightell, a former Special Forces staff sergeant, had a chiseled face shaped like that of a then-unknown comedian named Jay Leno. In fact, not only was Jay not a comedian yet, he was still a class clown, as it was early 1967.

"Hey, Bendell," Buck said, "Lieutenant Jones wants you in his office ASAP."

"Thanks, Buck," I said.

I put my Brasso, Q-Tips, and buckle back in the footlocker below my bunk.

Saying to Strandberg, "I bet I get chewed out for using too much shaving cream," I grinned broadly as I stood up on the metal frame of my bunk, walked along it, climbed onto the dressertop, and grabbed the transom above the door.

This practice of not touching the floor of our rooms was a common practice among all the candidates and saved additional hours of spit-shining the floor. Pieces of Kotex pads under the corners of all the furniture was another tactic we employed.

I swung out into the hallway, my stockinged feet landing on the four-inch-wide rubber runner. I scrambled down the hall, positioned myself in front of the tac officer's door, and knocked loudly.

Inside, Lieutenant Jones said calmly, "Come in, Bendell."

I panicked. No harassment! Something must be wrong!

Barely twenty years old then, I walked in the door, strode over to the tac officer's desk, and saluted sharply, saying, "Sir, candidate Bendell reports!"

The big lieutenant returned my salute and nonchalantly said, "At ease, Bendell. Relax, I didn't call you in here to harass you. We need to have a serious talk off the record."

Oh, no, I thought. Mom or Dad got killed in an accident. Something's wrong; maybe my sister or brother. He hasn't made me do any push-ups.

"Sir, candidate Bendell. Has something happened with my family, sir?"

"No, Bendell, nothing like that," Jones replied, and with a cool appraisal said, "Relax, and dispense with the 'sir, candidate Bendell' shit. Just stand at ease and use normal military courtesy. Do you know why I harass you men so much? Do you know the reason for all the inspections, spit shines, push-ups, work, harassment, lack of sleep?"

Spreading my legs and folding my hands behind my back, I said, "Yes, sir. You're separating the wheat from the chaff. You only have six months to make leaders out of us, and there's a war going on. We will be responsible for other people's lives."

"Partially," Jones said. "We also put each of you in

leadership positions and gave you a number of chores to accomplish, too many to accomplish. That was three months ago. You may not notice it, but each of you has learned now to accomplish as many chores by prioritizing, organizing, and delegating authority."

"Yes, sir," I replied.

Jones said, "Look, you have leadership qualities, Bendell, and I think you have a chance to make a good officer someday, but you just aren't ready yet. The thirteen-week board convenes next week, and I want you to take a voluntary recycle. You can start over in another company and graduate as a second lieutenant. If not, I'm going to have to take you in front of the board and boot you out."

My stomach dropped, but I just couldn't give up.

I was in shock, but I said emphatically, "No, sir!"

"What the hell do you mean, 'no sir!'?" Jones said. "Bendell, I'm giving you a chance to graduate. If you don't take a voluntary recycle, I have to kick you out. Do you understand?"

"Yes, sir, I do," I replied, "but I came here to be an officer. That's my mission. You might kick me out, but I will not quit, period."

Jones sat behind his desk, shaking his head from side to side, but I really meant it. I decided I was going to make it right then and there, or fuck it. All through my teenage years I made the wrong choices, but that day I just plain decided to grow up.

He spoke, "I just don't understand this, Bendell. Look at this."

He handed me a piece of paper, which I looked at. At the top it said, "Observation Report." It had been written by the candidate I grabbed by the seat of the pants and scruff of the neck and shoved through the hole through the barbed wire. It stated that I used foul language, an offense that can get a man kicked out of OCS. I finished reading it and handed it back to the lieutenant.

"Have you seen how bad your grades are, Bendell?" Jones said. "And your leadership rating is really bad. Look at that OR. You used vulgar language on the live fire exercise. I heard you. That's a major infraction, Bendell. Wake up and smell the coffee. Now, what do you have to say about that? Are you going to take a recycle?"

"No, sir," I said firmly. "You'll have to kick me out, but I will not quit. He had a right to write that OR on me. You tell us to write ORs on each other, sir, but I had a mission to accomplish, and I couldn't get men to assault an objective by saying, 'Now, gentlemen, let's go, please.' I also know my grades are bad, sir, but I didn't think my leadership was that bad. In any event, sir, I promised my dad the next time he sees me, I'll be wearing a gold bar. If that doesn't happen, it will be your choice, not mine. I will not quit."

Lieutenant Jones said, "I give up. I gave you your chance. Get out of here, Bendell."

My heart sank, but I snapped to attention, said, "Yes, sir," executed an about-face, and zipped out the door.

I headed straight down the hallway in the direction of my room but turned right into the latrine. I fought not to speak or show any emotions to the several candidates I passed along the way. In the latrine, I went into a commode stall, locked the door, and burst into tears. Facing away from the door, I pounded my fists on the wall time after time, until I finally noticed blood spots appearing on the off-yellow smooth tiles. Tears flowed freely, and I sobbed openly, silencing myself when I heard a candidate entering the latrine. The man left and I cried some more, releasing months of stress and tension. I couldn't help myself. It was the biggest disappointment of my lifetime, and I was a practicing alcoholic at the time, but hadn't been able to have a drink for several months. The door opened again, and I heard the voice of Buck Lightell again.

Lightell yelled, "Bendell, you in here?"

"Roger," I answered. "What's up, Buck?"

"Lieutenant Jones wants to see you in his office ASAP," Buck said.

"Thanks," I responded, tearing off toilet tissue to wipe my eyes.

I ran to the sink, sprinkled cold water on my face, checked the mirror after drying, and headed toward Jones's office.

Jones was still behind the desk as I once again entered and reported to him.

"At ease, Bendell," he said. "Know what these are?"

He held up three typed forms.

"Sir, candidate Bendell, no, sir," I replied loudly.

Jones handed the papers to me and said, "They are three more ORs written about your performance on the live-fire FTX the other day."

"Three more?" I asked, totally unnerved.

Jones smiled and said, "Yeah, written by Lieutenant Tarr, Captain Douglas, and me."

I gulped and said, "The company commander wrote an OR on me, sir?"

"Bendell," Jones responded, "that was some of the most outstanding combat leadership I have ever witnessed. Lieutenant Tarr and Captain Douglas felt the same way. Your grades are bad, but not that bad. You're about in the middle of the class, so there's a lot of room for improvement, but your leadership rating is one of the highest in the whole company."

I was dumbstruck but recovered enough to ask, "But sir, why did you try to convince me to take a recycle?"

Jones grinned and said, "To see how bad you wanted to make it. I don't want to produce officers that are going to get people killed in Nam."

"What if I would have taken the recycle, sir?"

"I would have let you," Jones replied. "You would have deserved it for not sticking to a mission and accomplishing it. What are you grinning at, Bendell? Do you think I'm funny-looking or something?"

"Sir, candidate Bendell, no, sir," I replied.

"I said, what are you grinning at, Bendell?" Jones asked.

"Sir, candidate Bendell, nothing, sir."

"Are you calling me nothing?" Jones queried.

"Sir, candidate Bendell, no, sir!" the smiling young man responded.

"You're still grinning, Bendell," Jones snapped, "I think you are laughing at me. Get outside and low-crawl back and forth across the company lawn until my arms get tired and sore."

I would have low-crawled across Siberia and licked the snow for nourishment, laughing all the way.

Still beaming with a broad smile, I said, "Sir, candidate Bendell, yes, sir!"

I snapped to attention, wheeled, and ran out the door. In the hallway I headed for the front door, bounded down the outside steps, and dove for the lawn. Still smiling, I scrambled across the wet grass on my elbows, knees, and belly, lawn sprinklers dousing me. My roommate, candidate Strandberg, walked out the door, still spit-shining one of his jumpboots.

He gave me a funny look and said, "Bendell, what are you laughing about?"

I looked up from my wet exercise field and said, "Karl, if you are doing something you believe in, never, ever, ever give up, no matter what happens, or what you are told!"

Completely drenched and covered with mud and grass stains, I laughed even harder as I slithered through the grass. Karl just shook his head from side to side, turned around, and walked back into the barracks.

My arms and legs wore out more quickly because of the water from the lawn sprinklers, and I soon felt like I was dragging a five-hundred-pound block behind me while I crawled, but I just didn't care. While I skimmed across the wet grass, my thoughts went back to my senior year at Tallmadge High School near Akron, Ohio, just a year earlier. I had been "class clown" at Tallmadge, and before that, nearby Coventry High School. Product of an unhappy youth and a broken home, I was a teenage alcoholic and looked at myself as a loser. The deep-seated tears, however, had always been hidden behind a veil of laughter and jokes.

At that time I didn't realize it, but the stand I had just taken with my tac officer was the turning point in my life. I started looking at myself as a winner from that point on for the rest of my life, no matter what has ever happened to me. Low-crawling through that wet grass, my arms and legs shaking from complete exertion and thinking I couldn't make another foot but still continuing to, somehow, I experienced one of the happiest, proudest moments of my life. I passed into manhood as simple as that.

That's also when I decided that I would wear a green

beret on my head right after I graduated and got a gold bar. Nothing would keep me from either goal. Crawling, with my strength quickly waning, I looked beyond my company barracks and watched the young paratrooper trainees across the street at Fort Benning Airborne Training School. In "tower week" they were being raised up by cable, three at a time, in fully inflated parachutes attached to the big mesh screens sticking out from the two-hundred-foot "jump towers." Three men were raised, with one cone, on the downwind side of each tower, always empty. Reaching the top, the parachutes released and the young airborne trainees dropped to the ground. I pictured myself wearing jumpwings and a green beret and jumping out the doors of exotic aircraft all over the world. I just knew it would happen. I would just simply not give up while others fell by the wayside.

That afternoon I got a one-hour pass, went to the PX, and bought a pair of jumpwings and the Special Forces crest with the words *De Oppresso Liber* on it. I pinned them both into the headband straps inside my shiny black helmet liner. They were pinned next to the shiny gold bar I already had hidden in there, and every time the going got too rough, I would remove my helmet and look at the reminders of my goals.

2

‒‒‒

Predeployment

Major Koga never smiled; in fact, he intimidated all
the young lieutenants with his straight talk and bore-
through-the-back-of-your-head stare. Even up there in the
blue Virginia sky, I could see those dark Hawaiian eyes
drilling into my own, but this time they were glaring. The
two of us were going to collide in midair, which I wouldn't
have minded if I were the one with a star over his jumpwings with a wreath around it. I subconsciously reached in
my fatigue shirt and touched my green beret, gold bar on
the red flash on it. Satisfied, I grabbed the nylon web risers
on the front of my parachute and climbed the lines as
quickly as I could. Major Koga, still staring daggers, passed
lower than I, and I saw that I was about to crash into the
side of the major's canopy. I pulled down hard with both
hands, my legs slipped up over the edge of the parachute,
and I ran across the top of the canopy. My own canopy
partially deflated as the other passed beneath me, but filled
with air when I ran off the other side. I quickly checked my
reinflated canopy to ensure that I didn't have any malfunc-
tions. It was fine, and I pulled on one riser and turned, to
see Major Koga facing me again. Embarrassed, I smiled at
the field-grade officer and wiped my brow.

Frowning, Major Koga yelled back, "Watch where the
hell you're going, Lieutenant!"

Pretending to be out of earshot, I nodded my smart-alecky head and muttered under my breath, "Fuck you very much, Major."

The ground got closer, and I pulled down on the right front riser, turning my chute so I faced into the wind. I saw one of my buddies about fifty feet away. The man waved, and I pointed at his canopy. He looked up to see he had a "Mae West"—one of the nylon suspension lines had crossed part of his MC-1 in the back, causing the chute to have two canopies, one large and one small. He shook the risers violently, and the line fell off the parachute. It blossomed into one parabellum shape. Technically, the Army required paratroopers to pull their reserve parachute immediately in the case of a Mae West; however, most Special Forces men and some other troopers usually chose to try to shake it out first. Army reserve parachutes don't have a little pilot chute, so you grab a handful of nylon and throw it out into the wind. There is always a chance that it can tangle with the main parachute and cause a "cigar roll" or "streamer," almost always fatal.

I looked down at the so-called drop zone to see which way the smoke blew from the green smoke grenade dropped on the ground. The wind was almost perfectly still, so I turned the parachute toward the deuce-and-a-half truck that was functioning as the turn-in point. The MC-1 or T-10 steerable parachute has an eight-knot forward movement in no wind because of the large oval vent in the back of the canopy. I moved toward the truck on the ground and wondered which of the many trees dotting the DZ I would crash into. The landing was uneventful, however, except that Major Koga was dropping onto the same forested field.

Jumping out of the old World War II–vintage CH-21

helicopters, which looked like giant, olive drab bananas, was a good diversion for me and the other members from Company C, 7th Special Forces Group. Normally stationed at Fort Bragg, North Carolina, the detachment had been in the woods of Camp A. P. Hill, in Virginia, for four weeks already. The men wore their green berets, but instead of jungle fatigue uniforms and jungle boots we all wore black pajamas and tennis shoes.

Every combat unit in the Army was required to participate in annual training exercises in which they were graded on their combat-readiness and efficiency. Even the Old Guard, Washington, D.C.'s, 3d Infantry Regiment, which supplied all the spit and polish in the nation's capital, had to participate. So men who normally guarded the Tomb of the Unknown Soldier, performed military funerals at Arlington National Cemetery, and handled all the other drill and ceremony functions in the area, had to trade in their shiny sabers for M-16's and head for the "boonies." A detachment of officers and NCOs from my unit at Fort Bragg were sent to Virginia to help train the men and to serve as an aggressor force during the field training exercise.

The 3d Infantry still had to perform their functions around Washington, so they sent their troops into the field one company at a time. Each company stayed for one week, and our Green Berets attacked them day and night, hid in tunnels in a mock Viet Cong village, and let them try to locate our hiding places and tunnel entrances as we hid from the American soldiers in the woods and swamps.

I still wore burn scars on my face from an experimental gas grenade that somebody had gotten his hands on and threw into a tunnel below the mock village; unsuspecting me crawled right into the gas. A CBN[1] investigation team was sent down immediately from the Pentagon and discovered the grenade but was totally puzzled about how it got into someone's hands. A device used to test the air in the tunnel where I got burned registered the gas as on the border between CS and mustard gas.

I was amazed by the extremely unusual accident, because I still bore the slight white hairline scar on my right cheek from a ricocheted M-14 bullet that had wounded me almost a year earlier, at Fort Dix, New Jersey. A soldier in AIT, I was on a firing range shooting an M-14 E-2 automatic rifle with my training company when the freak accident occurred during a rainstorm. Because of the weather, all the trainees wore Army ponchos over their steel pots. The bullet that hit me was apparently deflected off a flash suppressor that had come loose from the barrel of my rifle. It deflected the bullet down, it hit a rock in front of me, flattened out, bounced back, making a razor-sharp cut along my cheek, and made a three-inch-wide jagged hole through the hood of my poncho. The weird happening made me an instant celebrity as all range firing was shut down at Fort Dix. While still a wide-eyed trainee who had been in the Army less than three months, I was interviewed by three generals and a number of field-grade officers.

By the time I went to Camp A. P. Hill and got gassed in the tunnel, the scar on my cheek was a thin white line that would eventually disappear. The other oddity about the whole thing was that between A. P. Hill and Fort Dix, I also had another freak accident, at Fort Benning, Georgia, during OCS. The doctor who treated me at Martin Army Hospital told me that as far as he knew, I was only the

1. Chemical-biological-nuclear.

second person to get stung by a scorpion at Fort Benning. Falling asleep with all my other exhausted squad members on an ambush patrol, I got nailed on my right hand. It swelled up about five times its normal size, and I got sick as a dog.

A squad-size patrol from the 3d Infantry Regiment moved as quietly as possible down a trail in the middle of A. P. Hill. The last man in the squad, a tall private E-2 with black hair and glasses, pulled his final cigarette out of the Marlboro flip-top box. He also had two other boxes of the same brand in his other pockets. The squad leader halted the patrol as they approached the intersection of another well-worn trail.

"Okay, everybody be careful. There's another major trail crossing just ahead," the squad leader said, pointing to two squad members. "You go down the trail about twenty meters to the right, and you go down about twenty meters to the left. After we pass by, you two catch up."

"Aw shit, Sarge," a black spec 4 complained. "There ain't no fucking Green Berets within ten miles. They're all getting laid and drunk while we're out here humping the boonies, I bet."

"Shut up, Crawford," the buck sergeant said.

The patrol passed across the trail junction, and the last man tossed his empty Marlboro pack along the side of the trail. The two flankers saw this as they started to catch up but paid no attention, but the other watchers did. The squad moved out of sight down the trail and a man stood up out of the thick, green ground cover while another dropped from a tree over the junction. One second the two men were invisible, and the next second, they were both there. Both wore black pajamas, tennis shoes, and green berets.

The bigger man opened the pack, reached inside, and extracted several folded pieces of paper. He read them, laughing all the while.

The other said, "What's going on, man?"

The bigger man said, "You didn't recognize that last soldier in the patrol?"

"No," the other said, "I couldn't look up. They were so close I almost got stepped on."

The bigger man said, "You remember seeing that new tall, black-haired second lieutenant who came to the company about two months ago?"

"Wears glasses?"

"Yeah, that was him. The S-1 shop cut him phony orders two weeks ago, with a phony name and rank. He infiltrated the company in Washington and drops us messages at major trail intersections in empty Marlboro boxes," the larger NCO said. "We give them to Lieutenant Bendell or Sergeant Holland. He writes down their call signs, radio frequencies, and op plans. I forgot you just came up from Bragg."

The other man laughed and slapped his leg.

Astounded, he said, "We infiltrated a second louey into their company as a private before they even came to the field?"

"Fucking-A," the other replied. "Even pulled KP and guard duty."

The sergeant laughed again, saying, "Son of a fucking bitch, man, only in SF."

S. Sgt. Bobby Stewart, Sfc. Jim Hale, and I lay side by side on little nylon ponchos stretched between trees. We all smoked cigarettes, staring at various cloud shapes forming high above the sheltering trees.

I said, "Sergeant Hale, you sure the legs[2] can't find this guerrilla base?"

The E-7 smiled and replied with his lazy voice, "Relax, Thieu-uy,[3] I told you—old man, hair growing thin, many years, many stripes, you listen, you learn."

The younger team members in the hidden guerrilla base laughed as the balding NCO continued, "Lieutenant, we located this guerrilla base in the mortar impact area. There is no fucking way whatsoever that any of those leg officers is going to let their troops into a danger area like this."

Several 105-millimeter howitzer rounds exploded nearby as all the team members dived for the ground, crawling next to the nearest tree trunks. The two senior NCOs smiled, climbing back into their nylon hammocks almost before the echoes stopped.

Bobby Stewart spoke this time. "No sweat, you guys, we're so close to the edge of the impact area the chances of a round hitting close to us are smaller than a flea's dick."

I asked, "Where was Sergeant Holland going to locate the other guerrilla base?"

Hale replied, "A couple of guys found a patch of woods that belong to some farmer off the post. There wasn't any sign of people being around, so we ought to be able to hide there without being discovered."

Bendell laughed. "You know, since I'm the only officer, I'm going to get hung if we get caught setting up our guerrilla bases in all the areas where we are told to stay out of."

2. Nonparatroopers.
3. Vietnamese for Second Lieutenant.

Sergeant Stewart chimed in, "Lieutenant, this is Special Forces. We are trained to break rules and use our initiative. Besides, we need safe places to rest when we ain't harassing the legs, and furthermore, sir, who gives a shit if you get fried? You're an officer."

All the NCOs chuckled.

"Relax, Sergeant," I replied. "I didn't say we couldn't do it, I was just whining about it."

Stewart looked over and grinned.

I grinned and added, "Oh, yeah, I forgot. Fuck you, eat shit, and die, Bobby Stewart."

The E-6 chuckled heartily and took a big drag on his cigarette, blowing smoke up toward the far-off giant cloud formations.

The two trail watchers came into the guerrilla base and handed me the Marlboro box. I pulled the messages out, read them, then handed them to Sergeant Hale. On the ground I spread out a map covered with combat acetate.

"Hey, come here, guys."

The eleven other men in the guerrilla base gathered around me, some carrying canteen cups of hot coffee. I pointed to the map as I spoke.

"You men remember the second hill that we booby-trapped, over here on the west side?"

A number of the guerrillas nodded in understanding.

I continued, "They apparently decided on that spot to set up their new company perimeter and patrol that AO.[4] We need to book it on over there and pay them a little surprise."

An hour later, the twelve men watched, with binocu-

---

4. Area of operations.

lars, from the deep woods as the 3d Infantry Regiment company came upon the numerous leaflets attached to trees all over the hilltop on which they had chosen to locate. The SF team booby-trapped a number of hilltops every time a new company came to Camp A. P. Hill for their training. We simply picked likely spots, based on terrain and location, for the units to establish an operating base. We thoroughly enjoyed watching the new troops arrive as they yanked leaflets off of trees, unaware that the leaflets were connected to booby traps with little pieces of commo wire taped to the back. We also always left two smoke grenades at each location, which looked like they were dropped on the ground. In actuality, the grenades were connected to an explosive booby trap buried just underneath them. On top of that, there were trip wires, along with various rocks and sticks that just happened to be in the way.

The "snake-eaters" couldn't hear what was said but could imagine, anyway, as we watched and listened to various smoke grenades, artillery simulators, and other pyrotechnic booby traps being detonated. We also knew that the major wearing the white armband, the referee for the field training exercise, would declare that so many men were killed in action and another number wounded in action. The company commander would surely call for a medevac to evacuate the wounded soldiers.

Bobby Stewart said, "Hey, Lieutenant, they're bound to have designated wounded and called for a medevac, but we don't have choppers available."

"Yeah?" I replied.

"So they send an ambulance out to simulate a medevac," Bobby continued, "and we kind of hitchhike a ride into their perimeter and blow the fuck out of 'em all."

"He's SF, ain't he, sir?" Jim Hale interjected, laughing. "Kill 'em all, and let God sort 'em out!"

All the team members laughed.

I got excited at the prospect and said, "There's only one forest road coming into that hilltop, along that flat ridge there, isn't it?"

One of the younger sergeants on the team, a red-haired engineer/demolition specialist, said, "Fuckin' A, sir. I was patrolling on it this morning. It comes in from the highway and runs the entire length of the ridgeline. There're trees all along it and plenty of good ambush sites."

I watched the company through the binoculars for a few more seconds, then spoke. "Good idea, Sergeant Stewart. Why don't you take point and pick out a good spot for us to hijack the ambulance."

Stewart smiled, grabbed his gear, and took off through the woods at a killing pace. We followed.

The team followed the wiry NCO as he dodged bushes, branches, vines, and rocks. He wound around the hilltop, finally emerging on a double-rutted dirt road running east and west through the thick woods. Not stopping, the sergeant turned away from the company's location and moved quickly down the road. All the team members breathed heavily, and we were soaked with perspiration. A quarter of a mile down the hardpack, Bobby Stewart called a halt.

Taking a swallow from my canteen, I moved up to the patrol leader.

Pointing, Bobby said, "Sir, if we can rig two trees there and there to fall, in front of and behind the ambulance, we got 'em slicker 'n shit on a doorknob."

I just grinned and said, "Sergeant, this is your patrol. Go for it."

Bobby barked orders as team members spread out and prepared the ambush site, four of them cutting two small-trunked but leafy trees, using giant razor-sharp knives. Within minutes the two large saplings were cut almost through and had several ropes tied to each. Both lined the road, about fifty feet apart. The rest of the team members created and camouflaged hiding places next to the road, on both sides, between the cut trees. One man was sent seventy-five meters down the pathway in each direction, and the team sat down to wait. Most lit cigarettes and thought of combat, hoping Bobby Stewart's assumption would come true. It did.

Fifteen minutes after the spot was prepped, a whistle of a bobwhite quail filtered through the forest growth and all cigarettes were snuffed, weapons grabbed. Seconds later, a green Army ambulance drove carefully around the bend in the rough road. Stewart made a slight clicking sound, and two ropes were pulled. The farthest tree swayed, creaked, and fell across the road as the medic/driver slammed on the brakes. The other tree fell behind it, and men appeared out of the ground, as if by magic.

My adrenaline pumping and heart beating in my temples and eardrums, I jumped up on the running board on the passenger side of the three-quarter-ton ambulance while Stewart jumped up next to the driver's door, shoving the barrel of his M-16 under the man's left ear.

Teeth clenched, Sergeant Stewart said, "Boy, you ever slide a section of a cleaning rod down the barrel of an M-Sixteen, then fire it with a blank?"

The medic, teeth chattering, answered, "No, sir."

Bobby continued, "Don't call me 'sir.' I work for a living!"

I laughed and said, "Thanks a lot, Sergeant."

Stewart chuckled and said, "Sorry, Thieu-uy, no offense."

He continued, "Last week we needed some meat, so I shot a farmer's cow with a cleaning rod. Went clean through its fuckin' rib cage. You do exactly what I tell you, and my cleaning rod won't penetrate your little fucking leg brain, okay?"

"Yes, sir, uh, yes, I promise. I swear! Anything you say!" the driver/aid man declared.

"Turn off the engine," Bobby ordered.

The man complied, and a pair of handcuffs appeared in the NCO's hand. He closed one of the cuffs around the medic's wrist and the other around the steering wheel. The medic looked at the iron bracelets in shock, then, eyes wide, stared at the black-pajamaed sergeant. Bobby lit a Lucky and stuck it in the medic's mouth. Jumping off the running board, he ran to the back of the van. I met him there and laughed as I watched Bobby wink, pull the magazine for his M-16 out of a pocket, show it to me, and put it back in his pocket.

"Cleaning rod?" I said sarcastically.

"Got his attention, didn't I?" Bobby said.

This time *I* winked.

The rest of the team didn't need direction. Each man piled into the back of the ambulance, holding his weapon in one hand and a smoke grenade, pin-pulled, or an explosive artillery simulator in the other. Bobby Stewart climbed in behind the driver's seat and stuck his barrel up behind the man's head.

The sergeant spoke. "Wanna be a cow?"

The medic shook his head quickly from side to side.

Bobby said, "Drive. When you reach the company perimeter, drive right into the middle of it, stop the ambulance, and shut her down. Got it, son?"

The young man nodded his head affirmatively. He started the vehicle and took off for the guerrillas' objective. With a prod from Stewart, he turned on the flashers and siren.

The company stared as they heard the approaching siren. It died as soon as the big ambulance pulled into the clearing and entered the hasty perimeter the company set up. Most of the soldiers returned to their chores, digging foxholes, latrines, and building a command post bunker. As directed, the medic/driver stopped the big van in the center of the security circle and shut the engine off.

The back doors flew open, as did the right front door, with green beret– and black pajama–clad warriors jumping out, throwing smoke grenades and pyrotechnics in every direction around them. The Special Forces ambushers dived under the ambulance and opened up on full automatic with our M-16 rifles, with the big buck sergeant engineer firing all about him with an M-60 machine gun. Shell casings from the blank bullets piled up around us like copper snowflakes in a blizzard.

The soldiers of the Old Guard were off-guard. It took several seconds for most men to realize what was happening, and even more time to get their hands on their weapons and into play. By that time the Green Berets had already dropped numerous empty magazines on the ground all around them. On top of that, colored smoke swirled skyward in every direction around our guerrilla force, masking our positions, while we, closer to the grenades, could more easily see the 3d Infantry troops' positions.

For the most part, the entire episode was nothing but a mass of confusion and chattering weapons in the minds of most of the Old Guard soldiers. The incident happened so quickly, and we were hidden so effectively under the big ambulance, plus guarded by a protective smoke screen, that the leg troops were decimated by firepower from the Green Berets without returning any effective resistance.

The 3d Infantry company commander, very red-faced, stormed across the clearing, directing orders at men milling about here and there.

"Surround those men! Hold your weapons on them!" he shouted, then, storming toward us, continued, "You are all prisoners! Lay down your arms!"

The "snake-eaters" laughed heartily, and I hollered back, "Fuck you, eat shit, and die, Captain! You are one dead son of a bitch, and so are all your men! We just kicked the ever-loving shit out of your company!"

Still fuming and quickly approaching the guerrillas, he grinned an embarrassed grin and yelled, "Yeah, well, we have you and your men surrounded and outnumbered, you insubordinate asshole! Lay down your weapons or suffer the consequences!"

I had an ego now and a green beret and so did my men, so we held our weapons up in a fighting stance as I replied defiantly, "You wanna take my men's weapons, come on and try, but you better get some reinforcements, you needle-dicked bug-fucker!"

The captain stopped short at the words of a major wearing a white armband: "Captain, that will be enough! There is no way you could order your men to surround them and take them prisoner. They just about wiped out what was left of your company, including you!"

The captain got very frustrated and finally said, "Sir,

what about his insubordinate remarks? He called me a needle-dicked bug-fucker!"

The major grinned, looked at the angry commander, and replied, "Right now, Captain, he can call you anything he can get away with. He's a Viet Cong, not an American!"

The angry company commander stared daggers at me, so I gave him the finger, with the rest of the team following suit. Several chuckles from the company commander's men could be heard.

I walked over to the major and said, "Sir, may we have about a fifteen-minute head start to get away from here?"

The referee smiled and said, "Sure, Lieutenant, you've got half an hour. Nice operation."

I smiled, nodded, turned, and signaled for Bobby Stewart to come over. The NCO ran over, M-16 carried smartly at port arms. He stopped and grinned. The major smiled at him and stared at the little medallion worn from a leather thong around Bobby's neck.

I said, "Sergeant Stewart was the brain trust and commander of this little sortie, Major."

"Nice going, Sergeant," the major said, still glancing down at the base of the NCO's neck.

Bobby smiled. "Thanks, sir, but it was a team effort."

He held the little medallion up and continued, "Buddhist prayer circle. Got it off a VC battalion CO, Major."

The major asked, "You kill him?"

Bobby Stewart beamed. "Fuck, yes, sir. I think he was a major, as a matter of fact."

The field-grade officer chuckled a little too hard and waved off the two smartass but hopefully charismatic "green-beanies." We took off at a fast walk, and the rest of the team fell in behind. Two team members automatically took off at a trot as point for the patrol, while the spit-and-polish soldiers watched our team disappear quickly into the woods.

The humiliated captain watched us leave, then shrugged it off as he remembered the greater embarrassment suffered by the previous CO. We had printed up leaflets and hung them throughout the woods for the 3d Regiment soldiers to find. We had learned and printed the captain's name, serial number, address, and wife's name. We also made disparaging comments on the leaflets about "gang-banging" his wife and getting "number one blow jobs" from her. On top of that, my team had infiltrated his company perimeter and even thrown smoke grenades and artillery simulators in his tent.

The company commander shook his head and laughed the incident off. He figured that he got off lucky. The week prior to coming into the field, he heard two separate stories about these maverick warriors from Fort Bragg. The first story he heard was about the commanding general of JFK Special Warfare Center, which had been renamed to JFK Center for Military Assistance because it sounded "softer." The two-button general had supposedly been in a meeting where another CG, the commander of the 101st Airborne Division, complained that Green Berets were getting too much publicity and were highly overrated. The CG of JFK Center was said to have gotten angry and challenged the 101st commander. He supposedly said that they could plan an FTX in a certain area of operations, and one A team of Special Forces would infiltrate through the division, into the division command post, and simulate killing the commanding general himself. According to the story, the team did, in fact, sneak past all the sentries, listening posts, MPs, and others. They tore all the operations maps off the walls and piled them and other papers in the middle of the division command center, then set it on fire. They also sneaked into the commanding general's tent while he slept, and using lipstick, wrote "KIA" on the CG's forehead and drew a red line across his throat. They also pulled the pin on two smoke grenades and wedged them under the general's mattress so they would detonate when he jumped out of bed. After they successfully got away from the burning division headquarters, the team climbed over a fence into a drive-in movie theater, where several carloads of sympathetic civilians waited for them. The Green Berets changed into civilian clothes hidden in car trunks, then sat down and enjoyed a double feature while the 101st Airborne Division combed the entire area looking for them.

The other story was about a similar adventure against a Marine Corps unit at Camp Lejeune. The details were slightly different, but the outcome was the same.

The captain wondered if the stories were true or rumor, not knowing that my team sergeant, M. Sgt. Mike "Hardcore" Holland, was one of the men in the operation.

The team arrived at their guerrilla base with a cheerful attitude and our adrenaline still pumping. I yanked out my map and simply grinned. The NCOs smiled, too, knowing I had mischief in mind. They all gathered around the map as I pulled out a grease pencil.

I said, "How would you guys like to totally fuck with our demoralized enemy?"

One of the sergeants laughed and replied, "Do Mouseketeer girls have tight cunts, Lieutenant?"

I pointed on the map with the pencil.

"The company was here when we left them. I figure we need to allow ten minutes for everyone to figure out what the hell they should do next, and another ten minutes for the company commander to chew on everyone's ass. After that they would have struck their location and moved out for their transportation point, which is right here. It would take them about an hour and a half to hike there, maybe two."

Sergeant Hale laughed and said, "Sir, you ain't exactly being an officer and a gentleman. That spot where their vehicles are parked is off-fucking-limits. You want to hit them there, sir, right in front of God, a bunch of civilians, and everyone?"

I grinned broadly, tapping a Lucky Strike cigarette on the side of my shiny silver Zippo cigarette lighter. The tobacco, tapped down approximately one-quarter of an inch, met with my satisfaction. I made sure that the little printed Lucky Strike logo was near the end I would light, and I flipped the lid open by snapping my fingers over it. Then I snapped my middle finger on the striker wheel, and a flame shot up in front of my tanned face. I took three quick puffs without inhaling, then took a long, deep drag into my lungs and blew the smoke out of my nostrils in a steady stream of blue vapor. I coughed several times, feeling the burning in my lungs. I thought about the episode with the gas grenade when the previous company was at A. P. Hill, and put out the cigarette, field-stripped it, and whipped out a Swisher Sweet cigarillo, placing it between my lips. You don't have to inhale a cigar. Good thing I never had any superstitious habits either.

I stood up, grabbing my M-16 and ammo belt and harness. The others followed suit.

Bobby Stewart said, "The little store?"

I winked and puffed on the little cigar.

Jim Hale assigned two men as point, and the patrol headed out for the Camp A. P. Hill boundary.

After a fast march, we found ourselves at the edge of thick woods looking across a blacktop, lined highway. A car whizzed by, but none was parked across the street at the little country store. Waiting for cars to pass by, and moving two at a time, the team members dashed across the highway and into the brown-shingled store. Within a few minutes we were all safely assembled inside. The store-owner, always thrilled to see Green Berets, handed each of us a Coca-Cola and a little bag of potato chips. Two of the men moved over into the side room and started to set up a rack of pool on the old slate-top table.

Hale said with a growl, "Knock that shit off, you two. We're at the office. This ain't recreation hour."

The two men set the sticks down quickly and walked over to the rest of the team.

"Drivers!" a young sergeant yelled, standing lookout at the door.

The team quickly and efficently walked past the store-owner and his blond assistant. I smiled at the assistant as I passed by. The team ran up a short stairway and tiptoed down the dark hallway on the private second floor. We entered a door at the end and walked into a small room. A redheaded NCO sat in front of an AN/GRC-109 radio and a hand-cranked generator. We called the powerful radio the "angry 109."

He smiled at the team and said, "Hey, sir, I've been able to reach Fort Bragg with this sumbitch. How 'bout somebody cranking this fucker for me and I'll try now?"

I gave him the shush signal and pointed downstairs.

The man grinned and said, "No sweat, sir. We already checked, and they can't hear us downstairs."

I said, "Good. Any news from Smoke Bomb Hill?"[5]

"Same old shit, Lieutenant."

"Did you guys get the truck souped up?" I asked. "We need it, and we can't get caught."

The sergeant said with a laugh, "I didn't think we would, sir. It's hard making the time with one of us working downstairs as an assistant and the other up here monitoring the one-oh-nine, but we finally polished her off this morning. It'll run the fuck outta anything the Army makes, 'cept maybe a Cobra chopper."

Three taps hit the floor, and the team filed out of the room and down the stairwell. After exchanging pleasantries with the storeowner, we went out the back door and headed toward his barn.

I stopped and spoke to the store assistant. "Sergeant, don't have time to visit, but I just wanted to tell you guys you're doing a good job on the commo, and the truck, too, from what I just heard."

I opened the door as the civilian-dressed NCO said, "Thanks, sir. Thanks a lot."

I smiled and ran out the back. The rest of the team flew through the barn door, all riding on a souped-up U.S. Army one-ton truck. Bobby Stewart slammed the brakes on, and I jumped in.

An Army jeep flew in the driveway, and a tough-looking redheaded master sergeant in jungle fatigues hopped out. It was our team sergeant, Mike Holland, who drove over from the main guerrilla base when he heard what we were going to pull off. He saluted me, and I returned it. I grinned and let him in the middle seat.

5. The section of Fort Bragg where the Special Forces were located.

I said, "Just can't sit there with op orders and pencils, can you, Top?"

He gave me a sarcastic sneer. "Fuck, ya gotta be shittin' me, Lieutenant. I'm SF. I hate fuckin' paperwork. I like pussy, cold beer, and fightin'."

I laughed and said, "Well, shit, let's go kick some ass."

He slapped Bobby on the leg and yelled, "Fuckin'-A!"

We took off down the highway, and Stewart slammed his foot down on the accelerator. The big truck screamed along the blacktop while the warriors on the flatbed in the back whooped and hollered. It roared around several cars as I climbed out the passenger window onto the back of the vehicle. Damn, I was gung ho and quite stupid in those days.

"Everybody lock and load!" I yelled above the engine and wind noise. "Pull the pins on smoke grenades and artillery simulators! They have their trucks parked in a shopping center parking lot! We'll approach them slow, throw our pyrotechnics, open fire on automatic, and get the fuck out of Dodge City!"

Sergeant Richardson, an E-7 with only five years in the Army, yelled, "Sir, aren't you going to get your ass hung for attacking them in an off-limits area?"

I just grinned and yelled back, "Suppose we don't do any of our fighting in Cambodia, Laos, or North Vietnam, huh, Sergeant?"

The NCO grinned and I continued, "Besides, you shouldn't be SF if you can't take a fucking joke!"

Several of the NCOs laughed and raised their rifles up as I waved and climbed back into the cab.

"They spend hours and hours teaching us how to break all the rules, don't they, Thieu-uy?" Bobby Stewart said as he downshifted and screeched around a corner.

I lit a cigarette and tried it. I jacked a round in the chamber of my M-16, making sure the selector switch was on "SAFE." I pulled the pin on a red smoke grenade and held the grenade in my right hand.

The three of us grinned at each other as we spotted the 3d Infantry Regiment company milling around vehicles about a quarter mile away. There were numerous cars, houses, and businesses around, too. Stewart downshifted and slowed the Army truck to about thirty miles an hour.

Holland said, "They'll send those two quarter-tons after us when we hit them."

Bobby chuckled. "Yeah, we'll let 'em, Top. Those little jeeps are going to get surprised as hell when they end up sucking hind tit behind this monster."

Several soldiers noticed the approaching vehicle but seemed to turn to other activities. The shopping center loomed closer, and this time soldiers noticed the Green Berets all over the back of the flatbed. Men started pointing and several ran toward vehicles while Bobby Stewart stomped on the gas.

The one-ton truck slid around the corner and zoomed down the entrance drive into the little shopping center's parking lot. Old Guard riflemen, eyes opened wide, scurried in all directions. The snake-eaters opened fire, and we threw pyrotechnics at the confused GIs. I laughed as my red smoke grenade landed underneath a half-loaded two-and-a-half-ton truck and red clouds of smoke billowed out while soldiers scattered away from the vehicle.

Bobby Stewart swung the truck in a circle and made tracks away from the big unit. The company commander was humorous in his antics and rantings.

Bobby suddenly slammed on the brakes as he heard a voice from the back screaming, "My beret!"

Bendell looked back and saw the two jeeps starting pursuit and numerous civilians pouring out of stores and staring in amazement. In the meantime, a young buck sergeant from the team hopped down, ran back, grabbed his beret off the pavement, and sprinted toward the truck. In the meantime, the team covered him with fire and threw a couple more smoke grenades toward the approaching jeeps. Bobby revved the vehicle and floored it, tires screeching, as the E-5 approached the back of the truck. Jim Hale rapped twice on the top of the cab as I saw the sergeant being swung onto the flatbed by the machine gunner. Jim gave me the thumbs-up sign. I was then treated to a sight I thought I'd never see. The big truck roared past a cruiser with two police officers in it, but they just stared, jaws agape. In the meantime, the two jeeps quickly fell behind the bigger truck, their governors flattening out their speed at fifty miles per hour. Bobby got us away from the area and slowed to the speed limit while everyone lit up cigarettes and congratulated each other.

We soon made it back to the little country store, but there was a different Army quarter-ton truck parked in front. Stewart hit the brakes and, still out in the highway, slid to a noisy stop in front of the store.

Two soldiers ran out of the store and I yelled, "Fuck you, leg pussies!"

Half of the team in the back flipped the two men the finger and a couple threw artillery simulators. The angry young GIs bravely jumped in their vehicle and started it while Bobby laid a respectable patch of rubber. The big truck roared down the highway and around a bend. Stewart downshifted and slowed quickly, turning into a dirt logging road. He ran down it until we were out of sight from the highway. Within seconds, the jeep flew past out on the blacktop. Bobby floored it in reverse and roared back out onto the hardtop road. He headed back to the store, and the team jumped off the back, wiping away the tracks as Bobby pulled it back into the barn.

Bobby came out and I yelled, "Beers are on me, men!" The guerrillas, laughing and joking, headed into the little establishment.

The little NCO wrapped his arm around the younger man and said, "Thieu-uy, you love kicking ass, just like I do. When you get to the Big Rifle Range Across the Pond, beg, threaten, wheel, and deal, but get your ass assigned to a unit with Montagnards. The Yards love to kick ass, too, and they're the best at it."

A month later, back at Fort Bragg, some buddies and I left a fifty-foot rappelling tower, where we trained in the early morning, and headed toward an obscure little white frame building on Smoke Bomb Hill. It was already getting hot and humid.

Entering the door, I felt the coolness of the air conditioning and looked at the attractive Vietnamese lady smiling at me. She was dressed in a white silk outfit with slits down the side and black silk pants underneath. A colorful parrot was embroidered on the front of the outfit, and the lady bowed to me.

Returning the bow, I said, *"Chiao Ba Eaujeri. Ba manh jioi, phai khong?"*

She replied, *"Da phai, toi manh jioi, Thieu-uy Bendell. Cam on, Ong. Ong manh jioi, phai khong?"*

I looked at my Vietnamese-language instructor and wondered if I was learning the language of the people or the aristocracy. This woman was Madame Nhu's sister, after all. In just a few short months I was to learn that I was indeed speaking the Vietnamese spoken only in college classrooms and government meetings. It would take me a week of being chuckled at to learn to speak Vietnamese like the peasants and common people.

After a year of adventures and training at Fort Bragg and around the country, I, like other SFers, developed an attitude about other members of the military. John Wayne was making the movie *The Green Berets,* based on Robin Moore's best-seller of the same name. Sgt. Barry Sadler's song "Ballad of the Green Berets" was a nationwide hit. Those in SF enjoyed a rare celebrity status in the midst of antiwar protestation and a divided country. Men bought us drinks and women treated us as heroes, offering their bodies a lot. Quite often, however, others in the military regarded the maverick warriors with jealousy. The men of SF laughed, because suddenly it seemed that every special unit in the armed forces wanted to wear berets of some sort. We made jokes about performing missions in Vietnam and having conventional units take credit for it.

That year of training would be a year of excitement and idealism. I and the clique of young gung-ho Green Beret lieutenants I trained with looked forward to our inevitable tours of duty in Vietnam. We spoke of Montagnards and Chinese Nungs, Laotian Mnongs and Cambodian mercenaries, and the rumored fighting ability of each group. We complained about protesters and praised the names of legendary SFers: "Fasty" Fastenheimer, General Joe Stilwell, Bull Simon, "Splash" Kelly, and many more. Each young officer thought himself invincible, but many of us—most of us, actually—would be dead within a year or two. A number more would be tortured in either bamboo cages or stone-walled Laotian or North Vietnamese prisons.

3

Yards

The time finally came, and yours truly found himself smoking a cigarette at two-thirty in the morning in Honolulu International Airport. I was halfway across the Pacific, headed toward a date with destiny. My uncle Roy Bendell had fought in the Pacific Theater in World War II and had won a Silver Star and a Bronze Star with V device.

Talking to me a few months earlier as I kept a vigil over my dying father, I listened intently as my favorite uncle said, "Don, you are about to go on an adventure that you will never want to go through again the rest of your life, but it will also be an experience you would never trade for any other."

The words haunted me. They still do: He was right. I was excited but sick to my stomach as well. I knew I would land at Bien Hoa Air Base, then go to Long Binh Repo Depot, or Replacement Detachment. I assumed I would go to 5th Special Forces Group headquarters in Nha Trang, but still I worried. What if the 101st Airborne needed lieutenants, I wondered, or the 1st Cav, or the 4th, 25th, or 1st Infantry divisions, all leg units? What if I got stuck with a desk job? I loved SF and could not imagine being assigned to a conventional unit. I wondered how long I would live. Would my promotion to first lieutenant come through? More important, I wondered if I would come through as a hero or a sissy when the bullets started flying. Silhouette targets don't shoot back, I used to say. The Americans were called to board the new jet.

I extinguished my cigarette, looked around at the darkness, grinned, and whispered to myself, "Nice of the Army to let me visit Hawaii for an hour in the middle of the fucking night. Beautiful sights and sounds. There's the moon and there's the tarmac, and oh, boy, I can almost make out the outline of a fucking palm tree. I'm glad I kept volunteering to go to Vietnam. This makes it all worthwhile."

An hour after arriving at the Long Binh Repo Depot, I felt shocked. I actually landed at Bien Hoa, was transported by bus to Long Binh, and had not been shot, bombed, or mortared. I received my orders and smiled. I was to report to headquarters of the 5th Special Forces Group in Nha Trang.

Ka-whump! Ka-whump! Ka-whump! Rockets exploded all around the big shelter at the replacement detachment. Men, eyes open wide in fear, scattered in all directions, running in and out of the big shelter, which resembled a half-constructed airport hangar, with only the roof completed. Lying on the ground, I realized there were only a few incoming rockets, and I grinned nervously, lighting a Lucky. I noticed several pairs of eyes looking at me and the green beret on my head, so I calmly got up, walked back over to my seat, and puffed away on the cigarette as if nothing happened. I was definitely scared, but the beret not only got me laid a lot and free drinks, it carried with it a macho mystique and a responsibility as well. I had to play the part.

When the C-130 Hercules four-engine transport approached the airport at Cam Ranh Bay, I got my first taste of a Vietnam-style landing approach. The aircraft circled the air base one time, and in order not to draw enemy ground fire, it banked sharply and nosed toward the ground, straightening out before the end of the runway. At the last minute, it landed. I felt as if I had just dropped ninety stories in an elevator shaft.

Three friends from Fort Bragg and I took a shuttle to Nha Trang and began processing into 5th Group. We soon found the Officers' Club, which was on the second floor of a large building. The three of us grinned and strutted proudly, each sporting brand-new silver bars, as we were all promoted to first lieutenant as soon as we reported in.

Reaching the top of the stairway, one said to me, "Well, Bendell, are you going to try the yell you used to do at the Armpit?"[1]

"I don't know."

The other said, "Bendell, you ain't got a hair on your balls unless you do."

We walked in the door and saw a packed club. A Vietnamese band on a small stage in the corner was attempting to sing an American rock and roll song in broken English. Warrant officers, lieutenants, captains, majors, and lieutenant colonels sat at numerous tables and the dark-colored bar. There was much talking, laughter, and gaiety. The three of us stepped into the room and stopped.

I said, "Do you suppose many of them have been at Bragg and will know what to do?"

One of the companions laughed and said, "Only one way to find out, if you have any hair on your balls, Don."

Letting my ego jump up, I grinned, then cupped my hands in front of my mouth.

1. Nickname for the 82d Airborne annex of the Officers' Club at Fort Bragg.

The entire room got silent and all stared toward the three of us when I started to yell, "Anybody who can't tap-dance is queer!"

The three of us, along with all the seated and standing men throughout the crowded room, did a simultaneous amateurish attempt at tap dancing quickly. The tapping noise was loud but lasted for just seconds. It was followed by thunderous applause and cheers from the drinking crowd. My friends and I didn't have to buy any drinks, but all three of us got quite drunk that afternoon.

We took a three-day COC, or combat orientation course in which the new people were taught not to wear after-shave on ambushes, how to speak politely to indigenous civilians and soldiers, and other niceties. From my C Team headquarters in Pleiku, I went to my B Team headquarters at Kontum, and from there I was assigned as the CA/PO-XO[2] at A Team 242 at Dak Pek. I had made it. If I lived, I would spend the next year among the Montagnards, and it became an instant love affair between me and that whole race of people.

This old boy fell in love, for some reason, with the lore and the legends of the American Indians before kindergarten. When my buddies and I played cowboys and Indians, I always wanted to be an Indian. I joined an American Indian fancy-dancing group when I was seven years old. With the others, including my older brother, Bruce, I was soon making my own costumes, war bonnets, hair roaches, and feathered bustles. By my teenage years I was lucky enough to be winning first place in Indian dancing contests, beating Native American youngsters quite often. I wore moccasins to school many times, and in grade school I carried a

---

2. Civil affairs/psychological operations-executive officer.

beaded headband in my pocket every morning. Not allowed to wear a headband to school, I waited until I was out of sight from my parents, put the headband on, wore it all day at school, then removed it before going back home. I dreamed of living in the 1800s as a brave in a nomadic western tribe; I still do. I started bow-hunting at seven years of age, and I read everything I could about the West.

When I was introduced to the Jeh tribe of Montagnards in June 1968, I had finally come to the realization of a lifelong dream. I was at home. The Montagnards were totally different from the Vietnamese and were a different race completely. Warriors, the men, wore loincloths, carried spears, knives, and crossbows, and spent most of their time hunting in the jungle-covered mountains of South Vietnam's rugged Central Highlands. The women wore only black wraparound skirts, called *atoks,* and were barebreasted and barefooted. Men and women alike wore numerous brass bracelets, earrings, and ankle bracelets as well as beaded necklaces. Living in bamboo huts in communal villages, they primarily ate mountain rice, rats, monkeys, and most living things from the tropical rain forest.

The Yards were family-oriented, noble, spiritual, and fun-loving. The Dak Pek A Camp was in the valley where the Dak Poko and the Dak Pek rivers intersected. Surrounded by the highest mountains and thickest jungles in South Vietnam, it was four miles from the border of Laos and totally inaccessible by any type of boat or road travel.

When I arrived at camp, I spent my first twenty-four hours full of adrenaline-pumping incidents, a veritable "fix" for Special Forces troopers. I had to take the body of a little dead Montagnard boy back to his father, a village chief. Blaming Americans for not saving their people, even if they brought them to the medics when they were almost dead, the angry villagers almost shot me until stopped by the chief. Luckily, we became friends that day. The Vietnamese Special Forces team tried to claim six prostitutes who came to the camp with me and Commo Willy, a boyish, good-looking young sergeant who was the assistant radio operator for the team. The American and Vietnamese teams had a face-off with weapons, with the VN finally backing down.

Commo Willy had traded a captured Soviet machine gun for the six whores, who had been paid for a week in advance. The team commander didn't really want them, but decided maybe they could be good barter to someone from the 4th Infantry Division for food or booze.

Special Forces was famous for trading and scrounging for all their needs; for example, the camp at Dak Pek was authorized to have fourteen .30-caliber machine guns, but we had fifty-two permanently emplaced around the perimeter. Authorized to have two .50-caliber machine guns, the camp had seven. The camp was authorized no tanks, but we owned an M-60 main battle tank. When I arrived, however, nobody had yet figured out how to transport it to Dak Pek. Many times, one captured AK-47, SKS, or RPG machine gun could bring an entire planeload of food to the team.

Still during my first day, I was assigned to go out on an operation the following day. One of the sergeants and I drove in a jeep to the camp runway in time to see a 4th Infantry Division LRRP team member being stuffed into an indigenous body bag that was too small. The seventeen-year-old boy had been stitched up the front by a machine gun, and his buddies, crying their eyes out, kept forcing his body into the plastic bag, only to have one arm or leg pop out and then another. The final adrenaline-pumper: That first day was when I ran almost headlong into a beautiful Montagnard woman, Ning, and we fell in love at first sight.

One incident in particular during those first twenty-four hours bespoke what my Vietnam experience would be like. I went around the camp just checking things out and looking around. When passing near the camp motor pool, I heard some laughter and saw a group of four drunken Vietnamese men. In their midst was a little Montagnard boy of nine or ten years old who had a bloody mouth and was being pushed from one to another. One of the Vietnamese, laughing sadistically, asked the boy a question, which I couldn't hear, and the brave young lad simply sneered and spit at the Vietnamese. The man started to kick the young warrior, who bravely stood facing the bully, ready to accept anything the four men were ready to attack him with. I was mad and quickly walked up to the group, and without speaking, picked up a piece of two-by-four laying across the top of a fifty-five-gallon drum. I whacked the leader across the abdomen and kicked the man in the face. Not letting go of the board, I swung back around and whacked another across the side of the head, then swung the board up between the man's legs. The boy stood next to me, fists balled, ready to take on all comers. The four would-be bullies were slow to move until I pulled out a Swisher Sweet cigarillo, lit it, and handed the two-by-four to the little boy. I laughed my head off while the young brave chased the screaming Vietnamese out of sight.

I suddenly felt a chill, as if I were being watched, and I looked up at the many little hills surrounding me. Each hill was girdled by bunkers containing the families of the Montagnard mercenaries in Dak Pek's strike force. Countless Jeh men and women were standing on the hills looking down at me, smiling, apparently having just witnessed my defense of the boy. I decided it would be smart not to mention the incident, but didn't know that the leader of the bullies, the one I struck first, was the cousin of Trung-uy Hoe, the camp commander of Dak Pek.

Only one day at Dak Pek, and I had already become close with the Montagnards. The Vietnamese had a different opinion about me, however, much different. I made some Vietnamese "lose face" and took the part of the *moi*, an expression meaning "savage" that the VN used for the Yards, but it translates better to the term "nigger."

I will never forget all those mixed thoughts and feelings I had on that day. There was fear and love, humor and wonder, sympathy and awe. I never had so many heart-pounding things happen to me in a twenty-four-hour period.

The following day, a Huey picked me up at the camp helipad and gave me the five-minute flight to the top of the mountain due west of our camp. Jim Mitchell, the team's assistant intelligence specialist, a dark-haired young buck sergeant who loved women, was due to go on R and R, and I relieved him. The other American I was with was a very friendly, happy-go-lucky, redheaded E-7 named Harry Boyle. Harry was the senior radio operator for Dak Pek, and he was good at his work, well liked by everyone, but was known for something totally different. Harry Boyle was madly, head-over-heels in love with his Latin American wife. He constantly showed her photograph to guys on the team, which I quickly learned, and would talk about her great beauty. He would always comment that he met her while assigned with the 8th Special Forces Group, headquartered in Panama but operating throughout South and Central America. She was in California and could not speak English, so Harry would always emphatically say that he just could not be killed, or she would be lost and all alone.

We were on one peak of a twin mountaintop. The jungle had been cleared away and bunkers had been constructed in a perimeter and all over the summit. The mountain directly to the south was occupied by a company from the 1st Brigade of the 4th Infantry Division from nearby Dak To. The next mountain south had another company and a 105-millimeter artillery battery, and the next mountain had still another company. Working opcon[3] to the 4th Division battalion, my unit was to provide flank security to the north and run small patrols and ambushes in an assigned area of operations.

There were one hundred Montagnard strikers, and the CIDG[4] company commander was a Cambodian named Mr. Lon. Although he was one of the tallest CIDG members at Dak Pek, he looked like he was Errol Flynn's shorter brother. The mountainsides were straight up and down, and the triple-canopy jungle was so thick and it drove you backward so much, that you could try to walk a mile, without help or a machete, and if you started on Tuesday, you would arrive the previous Monday.

Howitzer artillery 105- and 155-millimeter rounds came in big metal tubes with screw-on lids. They would fill up a helicopter load of the empty tubes with water at Dak Pek and fly them up to us. It was too hard and dangerous sending patrols down the mountain to the streams.

An incident on about my second or third day on the operation showed me that some of the indig (indigenous)

---

3. Under operational control.
4. Civilian Irregular Defense Group, mercenary fighters paid by Special Forces personnel out of a private checking account funded by the CIA.

did, indeed, have a sense of humor. We were all eating lunch one day, and I ate near the Cambodian Mr. Lon. He had a bunch of peppers lined up on a log and would pop one in his mouth every few seconds while he ate his rice. The interpreter was a fifteen-year-old father of two named Suet.

Through Suet I asked Mr. Lon if the peppers were very hot. He shrugged it off and shook his head "no." Friendly smile on his face, he offered me a pepper and I accepted it. I shoved the little hot ember in my mouth, took two bites, and gasped, mouth open, while Lon and the Yards roared with laughter. I ran to one of the canisters of water, spun the lid off, and turned the giant container up, pouring water all over myself and down my boiling throat. Drenched, I was finally able to chuckle at myself, too. I could tell the Yards liked that.

Later that day, Harry Boyle and I sat on a log with steaming canteen cups in our hands, staring into a fire. It was one of those things that men had been doing for hundreds of years and will probably do a few hundred years from now. We got on a discussion about a well-known SF master sergeant who served with me at Bragg and Harry in Latin America.

"Hell, yes, I know old 'Tightskin.' He was in South America with me," Harry said. "He was your team sergeant?"

"Yeah," I replied. "You know he's getting married for the fifth time?"

"No shit?"

"No shit," I replied. "You wouldn't believe what he'd tell each of us lieutenants back at Bragg if we got engaged."

Harry laughed and sipped his scalding hot coffee, saying, "Lieutenant, I'd believe anything anybody told me about Mike. What would he say?"

I chuckled and said, "First he'd lecture us and tell us women were all fucking mules and plugs and stay away from them. When he saw that that wouldn't work, he'd say, 'I'll tell ya' how ta' have a good marriage. When ya' leave fer work in the mornin' pat 'em on the ass, but when ya' git home at night, sock 'em, knock 'em down, and horse-fuck 'em, and show 'em who's boss.' "

Harry almost fell off the log laughing, and I joined in. Harry said, "That's Tightskin, all right."

I continued, "That's not all. He acted serious and if we laughed at him, he'd say, 'I'm not shittin', sir. I'm telling you how to have a good fuckin' marriage. I know what the hell I'm talkin' about. I been married four fuckin' times.' "

Harry and I had a good laugh over that. Then he told me about what the old SF master sergeant pulled on his last tour in Vietnam.

Harry said, "This really nice American missionary came over with his wife and daughter. The girl was a knockout, but she was only fifteen years old. Anyhow, Group assigned an E-8 to escort the family around Group headquarters and feed 'em shit. This E-8's showing them the sights, and Tightskin and another guy, an E-7, happen to pop in to Group right at that time. Both of them had been on an operation and hadn't shaved, showered, or changed for two weeks. The E-8 makes a big deal about them being war heroes, so he introduces them. Well, old Mike shakes hands with the missionary and his wife. Then he looks at the girl, holds his fist up like this, and grabs his elbow. Mike says, right in front of the parents, 'Hey, you're a cute little thing. You like to have a dick, about this big, shoved up that tight little cunt of yours?"

I spit hot tea all over myself and did fall over laughing.

I asked, "What the hell did the parents say?"

Harry laughed and said, "The guy that told me said that the mother actually fainted, but I find that hard to believe."

"Speaking of women," he added, "did I show you how beautiful my wife is?"

Harry reached for his wallet and I laughed again, saying, "Harry, I've seen her several times already. She really is a beautiful woman. While we're on the subject of beautiful women, do you know a woman down at the camp named Ning?"

"Hell, yes!" Harry said. "She's the hot mama of the camp along with her girlfriend, Mai, the one with the giant tits, lives right behind the dispensary."

I chuckled and nodded my head affirmatively.

Harry laughed and said, "I figured you spotted her. Tits like that are hard to miss."

I laughed and said, "Or forget."

I joked about Mai's physical endowments, but I could not get my mind off the tall, beautiful Montagnard girl named Ning. In fact, I thought, she had a nice, respectable pair of breasts herself; besides, I was a leg man, and hers started at the ground and went to paradise.

I dreamed of adventures in paradise.

I also thought of my newlywed wife back in "the world," and my ears burned with my own feelings of shame and guilt. I married one month before coming to Vietnam. My father died two weeks before that. It had been some year. I found myself starting to think about all the stupid rationalizations of being at war all the way around the world, and my life maybe ending at any minute. I knew I was trying to justify the fantasizing I kept having about the

Oriental beauty and me, but the line didn't really cut the mustard. If I let anything happen, I knew and believed it would be wrong, but I was young, alcoholic, and self-centered.

"Tell me about Ning, Harry?" I asked.

He replied, "I heard she and Mai were hooking with some Hundred-and-first Airborne soldiers when they were here at the camp."

I was surprised and showed it.

"Hooking? A Montagnard woman?"

Harry said, "I'm not sure. That's just what I heard. I know every man who looks at her wants to fuck her brains out, just about. I think she's taller than most 'cause I heard her dad or granddad was a French soldier. Her figure must be about a thirty-six, twenty-two, thirty-six. She is definitely a looker. Smart, too."

I thought back to the incident in my bunker before coming up on the mountain. It was the first night at camp, and I had eaten supper with my new friend Nhual and his family. He was the head interpreter for Dak Pek, and he had a nice wife and two small children. I had also been adopted, just about, by a little orphaned girl named Plar, who went to dinner with us in the tiny underground bunker.

Leaving Nhual's bunker, I took some tunnels back to our team TOC, walked up four steps into the concrete-sided four-deuce mortar pit, crossed it, then went down the four dirt steps to my bunker door. I heard a slight noise on the other side of the door, so I drew my .357 magnum out of the quick-draw holster on my hip and dived headfirst into the darkened room.

Ning flipped on the light switch and dropped her *atok* sarong. She wore only a smile and a small beaded string that went around her waist and dipped down above the very sparse triangle of black pubic hair. Harry Boyle's assessment of her having an hourglass figure was very accurate. She kissed me and tried to seduce me, but I couldn't let myself make love to her. Nonplussed, she left me with a promise that I would want her very soon. Her naked image haunted me and so did her impish smile, but the odd thing was that I thought of her laughing, intelligent eyes most of all. She always looked like she was teasing you and that her eyes were enjoying a private joke.

It was *poc* time,[5] and I was awakened by Suet, who ran into my little log and mud bunker.

"Trung-uy, come quick! VC! Come quick!"

Grabbing my little sawed-off CAR-15 rifle, I ran out the bunker door. Harry emerged from his bunker at the same time. We gave each other questioning looks and followed Suet to a foxhole on the perimeter toward Dak Pek. A very young Montagnard striker stood, white-faced, on the edge of his foxhole. He couldn't have been more than eleven or twelve years old, but with the Jeh, that could be manhood.

Suet had been hired as an interpreter because he had killed a Vietnamese in a fistfight when he was only twelve years old. At fifteen, the stocky little warrior had already been a husband and father for several years.

Suet spoke rapidly with the little frightened striker, and I wondered what was being said as the boy gestured excitedly toward the nearby thick jungle. Suet had a broad smile on his face, and it made me even more curious. Each of the thirty-one tribes of Yards had their own language

5. A two-hour nap everyone took all over Vietnam; the same as a siesta.

and customs, and most didn't speak Vietnamese, so I didn't have a clue as to what was being said.

Laughing, Suet turned to us and said, "This is first operation for this man. NVA soldier carrying AK-Forty-seven walks out of the jungle right down there and both men stare at each other. This man didn't know what to do, so he says to NVA, 'Are you a VC?' NVA runs into jungle. Now everybody will tease him *beaucoup.*"

I couldn't help it. I felt sorry for the young man, but I laughed hard, as did Harry Boyle. I had to try to figure some way for the embarrassed lad to save face, though. He looked crushed.

"Suet," I said, "I want you to speak loud, very loud. Tell him I said that he's very smart. I like to dress my point men up in NVA uniforms sometimes, and I have them carry AK-Forty-sevens. If they run into another NVA patrol, they can open fire first. He was smart, because that could have been a patrol I sent out, but tell him from now on I will always let everyone know if I send anyone out dressed like NVA."

Suet gave me a knowing smile and translated my words. I still couldn't understand the words, but the young man's chest puffed out and the expressions on the faces of his comrades spoke volumes.

We turned and walked back up the hill, and Harry Boyle gave me a sly smile, saying, "Lieutenant, you're SF."

My chest puffed out, too, and my shoulders seemed to go back a little more.

I winked and caught up with Suet, who had gone ahead.

"Suet," I said, "why don't you teach me to speak Jeh while we are up here on the mountain?"

He looked puzzled.

"Why, Trung-uy? We have good interpreters at Dak Pek."

"I just want to learn your language."

Suet smiled and said, *"Liem jai!"*

"What's that mean?"

"Means very good, number one, Trung-uy."

Harry Boyle left the next day and was replaced by his assistant, Commo Willy. Don Williams was born in Virginia, but his mother moved him to Florida when he was a teenager. He spent his first year in Vietnam with the 1st Air Cavalry Division but had been with SF for almost two tours when I met him. His father and every male member in his family had been killed in war, so he was bound and determined to prove to his mother, aunts, and cousins that there was not a curse on the men in his family. Commo Willy was fun. He worked hard and had a hell of a sense of humor. He always had a grin on his face like the little boy who stole Granny's pie off the windowsill.

The day after Commo Willy arrived on the mountain, I took a small patrol out and scouted north of our position. We followed a gentle ridgeline for a couple of miles and dropped into a deep ravine. We crossed one more ridgeline to the west and came out on top of the next, directly across from some rock cliffs near the top of the next mountain. Hidden in the jungle near the rocky cliffs were some caves and old French gold mines in which the NVA and local VC often hid.

Suddenly the eight Montagnards with me got their rifles ready to fire and crouched quickly into the jungle. I don't know how they knew to do so, or how they knew there was danger, but this was just the first of many times I witnessed this type of unexplainable behavior with the

Yards. Seconds later the two point men showed up, crawling on hands and knees.

Through Suet, they told me they ran into an NVA soldier carrying an SKS, and he dived into a bunker along the side of the trail. The two point men led Suet and me to a spot within sight of the bunker, with the rest of the patrol following, except for two men. I left them as a rear guard in case a patrol followed us, or we came under fire and had to make a strategic withdrawal. That's a retreat if the enemy's doing it, and a strategic withdrawal if you do it.

The bunker was along the side of the trail with steep jungle-choked mountain falling off on both sides of the trail. It was a camouflaged log and dirt bunker, which was barely visible with jungle undergrowth already covering it. If a machine gun crew were within, they could pin a unit down for a long time, so we lay there and just watched patiently for a long time.

Watching for half an hour, I spotted no activity, so I figured the NVA soldier either knew we were coming and waited patiently for us, or had crawled inside to look for a cache and simply left while the men came to summon me.

I was not a hero, just an insecure young man who was very gung ho because I loved emotional highs and getting recognition. As a commander, I had several options, but I told the Yards to stay where they were and chose an Audie Murphy course of action. I stripped off my ammo belt and harness, hung my little CAR-15 upside down across my back like a quiver of arrows, and handed my combat acetate-covered operations map to Suet. It had markings showing the locations of all our friendly positions, so I couldn't afford for it to fall into enemy hands.

"If I get killed or captured, burn that map and lead

the men back to Commo Willy," I said—as usual, being a bit melodramatic.

I called Commo Willy on the radio and let him know I was taking out a bunker with one possible NVA inside. I had one magazine in the rifle, and I shoved another in the left cargo pocket of my tiger suit. I grabbed two high-explosive hand grenades and carried one in each hand as I smeared some mud on my face and went down over the right side of the mountain.

Only a person who has tried to traverse the terrain in that area can appreciate how hard it is to move through it. The dark jungle is so thick that vines pull at your torso, legs, and arms. You cannot see more than five feet in front of you, and the mountainside I was moving diagonally across was almost straight up and down. I spent most of the time crawling on my hands and knees and had to estimate when I was even with the bunker.

It was only a fifty-meter distance, but it took me almost thirty minutes to arrive almost even with the bunker. I was covered with leeches, especially inside my shirt, but I couldn't think about such things then. When I peeked out from the jungle growth, I was only twenty feet from the front side of the bunker. I was visible from the firing port but figured the enemy within was not looking at the ground in front of the bunker. Chances are he was inside and occasionally looking out to see if anyone was coming down the trail.

I pulled the pins out of both hand grenades and held the Mickey Mouse flippers tight against the deadly little bombs. A grenade in each hand, I hugged the ground with my body and mentally tried to melt myself into the wet earth while I crawled forward on forearms, elbows, and knees.

I made it to the edge of the firing port, let the handles go, and held the grenades in my hands while I mentally counted, one thousand, two thousand. I tossed the deadly baseballs in the dark hole and heard a surprised voice and a metallic clicking sound from within. I took about two running steps, body leaning forward, and made a racing dive into the foliage with the bunker exploding behind me as I sailed into the tanglefoot and undergrowth. I rolled and rolled through the thick brush, forcing myself down until I finally came up hard against a sapling. Seconds later, dirt and pieces of bunker rained down on top of me.

I swung my CAR-15 around, checked the barrel for dirt, and scrambled back up the mountainside. Suet and the rest of the patrol met me at the demolished bunker. The top of it was blown out, but the biggest part of it collapsed in on itself. Thick logs stuck out of the wet, red-brown dirt. We saw no body parts but assumed the soldier was buried beneath the debris and mud. I stuck a Swisher Sweet cigarillo in my mouth and lit it while several Dega[6] poked around in the debris. One held up a loaded magazine from an SKS rifle and grinned at me. I called in a spot report to Commo Willy, which he relayed to the 4th Division. I just indicated that an enemy bunker was destroyed, as I hadn't seen the body.

We saddled up and headed back toward the barn.

Commo Willy and I spent another week on the mountain, at one point getting mortared by a company of NVA on the twin peak next to us. While Commo Willy ignored their fire and shot back at them with our 81-millimeter mortar, I directed mortar and artillery fire on their position from Dak Pek and the 4th Division. The NVA were

6. The Montagnards' term for themselves.

hiding in reinforced bunkers, so I had to call in TAC air on them. Jets came in dropping five-hundred-pound bombs and cluster bombs units (CBUs), but those were also ineffective. I had them bring in more jets and drop napalm, which wiped out the entire NVA company. Although the enemy simply hid in their safe bunkers during our counterstrikes, the napalm exploding collapsed their lungs, and those who survived that burned to death.

An incident happened while we were receiving incoming that brought home the fact that I was working opcon for a conventional unit. While we were still taking incoming mortar rounds from the NVA and I was trying to adjust indirect fire from several sources, I got a call on the Prick-25 from the battalion S-3[7] of the 4th Infantry Division unit.

I was in the middle of a battle, with my heart pounding and my mind running in little circles, wondering where the mortar round would hit each time I heard the hollow thunks from the other peak. I got a call from the 4th Division battalion headquarters two mountain peaks to my south.

Answering the radio, I heard the voice of the S-3 crackling over the busy airwaves: "Alpha, how many incoming rounds have you taken inside your perimeter so far, and how many have landed outside? Over."

I couldn't believe it.

Keying my mike, I screamed, "Get the fuck off the horn! I'll call you if I need you!"

I threw the microphone on the ground and pulled out a cigarette, lighting it. Everyone was hiding in their bunkers and foxholes, but I turned and looked at the laughing face of Commo Willy, who was busy still firing the .81 back

7. Operations officer.

at the NVA. He just shook his head from side to side and chuckled.

I grinned and yelled, "Hey, Sergeant, you wanna get killed? Those fuckers are shooting at us."

He just laughed some more and said, "Fuck it, nobody lives forever. You know that was a captain or a major you just cussed out."

I laughed and yelled back, "Oh, well, fuck it, nobody lives forever."

We both stood there, exposed to enemy fire, laughing at ourselves and our own misfortune.

The following day, the S-3, who turned out to be a major, flew out to our mountaintop. He treated me really nicely and asked for my assistance in determining where to locate the 4th Division ambush patrols. The whole time we talked, Commo Willy stood behind him and made faces at me, making gestures about me getting hung or shot.

Later that afternoon we drank coffee and I ate dehydrated chili con carne while Commo Willy ate dehydrated spaghetti and meatballs. The LRRP rations, I thought, were pretty good and beat the hell out of C rations any day. You just boiled a canteen cup of water over a fire and poured it in the plastic container of dried food.

Swallowing a bite of food, I said, "Tell me about Ning."

Commo Willy grinned and said, "I'd fuck her for a nickel and wouldn't care if I got paid. Of course, who wouldn't?"

"That's it? That's what you can tell me about her?"

"That's it, Lieutenant. Don't know much about her," he replied.

I made a cup of hot cocoa and offered Willy some.

I said, "Hear what happened to Harry Boyle and me before you came up?"

"Yes, sir, I heard you earned yourself a nickname."

Commo Willy roared with laughter while my face flushed with embarrassment. He was making reference to the morning I emerged from my bunker wearing an Army poncho liner with a neckhole cut in it, a camouflaged cowboy hat, a .357 magnum in a quick-draw holster, and a week's growth of beard.

I stuck a cigarillo in my mouth, lit up, and looked up at Harry Boyle, who said, "Clint Eastwood!"

I tried to look tough and spit, with the saliva dropping onto the toe of my jungle boot. Harry fell off the log laughing, and my nickname was born. I would not hear the end of it.

"No," I said, "that's not quite the story I was thinking about. I mean when we got overrun by the NVA regiment."

"Lieutenant, what the fuck you talking about?" he asked. "I went to Kontum for a few days, but I didn't hear about you and Harry getting in shit."

I took a swallow of hot cocoa and said, "Fuck, yes, it was horrible. In fact, it was when you were en route to Kontum; I remember hearing on the radio."

The young sergeant got excited and said, "So what the fuck happened?"

"Well," I went on, "Harry and I were sitting here drinking coffee, about the same as we're doing now."

"Did you get probed or what?" he asked, getting enthused about the story.

I went on, "No, we got fucking hit, big time. A whole fucking company swept up that ridgeline over there, right in the middle of *poc* time. There was a reinforced company acting as a blocking force over here, and a company-minus all along the perimeter down there toward the camp."

"Fuck," he said. "What about that side, toward Laos?"

"Oh, shit," I said, "they had another reinforced infantry company, with a lot of guys carrying B-40 rockets, and sappers with satchel charges. That's where the main attack came from. They spread out all along the western end of the perimeter and swept across the top of our FSB.[8] It was in-fucking-credible!"

Commo Willy's eyes were like saucers, totally swept up in the story.

"So what the fuck happened then, sir?"

I smiled, took a slow sip of hot chocolate, and said, "Well, we both got killed, of course."

Commo Willy stared at me a second, broke into a broad grin, then outright laughter.

"Hey, Lieutenant," he said, "fuck you and the horse you rode in on."

When I returned to Dak Pek, I spent a lot of time going out to Montagnard villages. Sixteen of them surrounded the camp, each on a cleared hillock. As an alcoholic, it was a great job, because I was always invited to get drunk with each village chief on smooth old Yard rice wine. They had large earthen crocks of fermented rice, with occasional potato peelings, rat pieces, and so on. I loved the wine but wasn't enthused about the usual meals of rats, bats, monkeys, snakes, dogs, cats, grubs, and other tidbits found in and around the adjacent jungle.

My primary job, other than killing bad guys, was to endear the Montagnards to the cause of freedom for the

8. Fire support base.

South Vietnamese, which was kind of like being ordered to convince the slaves in the early 1800s that they should fight their asses off to save the slaveowners and slave-traders from other slaveowners and slave-traders who wanted to steal their lands. Not only that, it was also like being ordered to get those same slaves to love and appreciate the slaveowners and slave-traders. The other part of the job was to propagandize against the NVA and VC, which was an easy task in itself. I simply had to expose us to the Yards and let the NVA and VC expose themselves to the Yards, and they knew whom to trust and believe in. The Vietnamese took away their lands, their rights, their peace, and their lives. The Yards hated, and still do hate, the Vietnamese, both North and South.

Most SF troopers had an inordinate amount of individualism, heroism, principle, and independence. That endeared them to the Yards, who respected all those traits. That is why the Montagnards are still some of America's staunchest, most loyal allies, even though we've screwed them over royally.

I was able to keep away from Ning about as well as a magnet could keep away from another with an opposite pole, especially after Harry Boyle, devoted and proud husband, got killed. Larry Crotsley, the team engineer/demolition specialist, dropped a booby-trapped .60-millimeter mortar round down the tube of a mortar, with most of the team watching. It exploded about fifteen feet out of the tube, killing Harry and a man from the 403d Army Security Agency instantly; blowing Larry over the berm of the bunker; seriously wounding the team medic, Dennis Afshar, in both arms; and wounding a brand-new man to the team, who died from a stomach wound a week later. I was in Nha Trang at the time.

In all fairness to my ex-wife, our marriage didn't have a chance in those days. It lasted ten more years after Vietnam, but came close to ending every day I was there. I was head over heels in love with Ning. I was in love with the little girl Plar and got the paperwork to adopt her, but couldn't get my wife even to discuss it in letters. Why should she, though? We had been married only a month before I went over. I was drinking continuously and hated everyone but the Montagnards, but there was one more thing sabotaging my marriage and chance for a normal life: When I was a boy growing up, I had an Indian name, "Wahpecan." It meant simply "Thunder." Some of the Montagnards were calling me "Bau Jah," which meant "Killer," or technically "Who Kills." My childhood dreams of dancing the great sun dance, counting coups, standing next to my breechclothed brothers while fighting our enemy in pristine wilderness, and returning to make love to my beautiful copper-skinned, raven-haired lover in my lodge—all those dreams had come true. I was in my own "happy hunting grounds."

We see movies with American Indians wearing eagle feathers in their hair, on their horses, in war bonnets, or on coup sticks. These eagle feathers were earned by counting coups. If a brave touched a live enemy soldier in battle, that was counting first coup; killing an enemy was second coup, sometimes first; touching an enemy someone else already counted coup on was counting second or third coup, depending on whether the enemy was alive or dead. Killing a grizzly bear was considered first coup.

I was counting coups, and I couldn't have been happier. I even bought a Bear Kodiak Magnum bow and quiver of hunting arrows on the black market in Kontum and got into bets with Montagnard men who used bamboo crossbows. We would set cigarettes up on sandbags and shoot for packs of American cigarettes or cans of beer. I even went out after a man-eating tiger that ate one of the village women. Of course I had a patrol of Yards with me, carrying rifles, grenades, and so on, so I wasn't exactly pitting myself against outrageous odds.

My involvement with the Yards got deeper and deeper, and they appointed me a brigadier general with the FLHPM of the FULRO movement. The FLHPM was an acronym for Front de Libération des Hauts Plateaux-Montagnards. This was a secret resistance movement comprised of Montagnards from each of the thirty-one tribes and was part of the trilateral FULRO movement. FULRO meant Front de Lutte Unifié des Races-Opprimées and was comprised of the Montagnard movement along with a Cambodian resistance movement, the Front de Libération de Khmer Krom, and the Cham people's resistance called the Front de Libération de Champa. The entire FULRO movement was headed by a Rade Montagnard named Y-Bham Enuol. The goal of the movement was to band together and try to get the Central Highlands returned to the Montagnards, as it was recognized as their lands and their autonomy was recognized, first by the French with an ordinance dated May 27, 1946; and after that, Bao Dai, Vietnam's last king, recognized their autonomy as well, in the early 1950s. Ngo Dinh Diem, South Vietnam's first president, however, really started a governmental policy of trying to push the Yards out of the Central Highlands and take the mineral-rich lands for the Vietnamese people. The Yards also were not given, and still don't have, a right to vote; representation in government, schools, or hospitals; or any other rights at all. Vietnamese soldiers would go into Montagnard villages and take food, money, and plunder in the name of taxation. They would also take women when they wanted and would pick out men with leadership traits, accuse them of being in the FULRO, and publicly torture and execute them.

Because of my association and support of the FULRO, the South Vietnamese in my camp started having various hired assassins try to kill me. Ning was hospitalized after drinking poisoned whiskey meant for me. She was cured but had some digestive problems for a while. They booby-trapped a jeep I was driving and the gas tank exploded, engulfing the whole vehicle in a ball of flames. I was able to dive out with just a minor scratch. One night, while I was on radio watch in our team house, they put a trip wire across my path just outside the door of the team house. It was attached to a booby-trapped cluster bomb unit. I stepped on it, but it didn't work. Our demo man, Larry Crotsley, and I sat on the sandbags of the .50-caliber machine gun nest above my bunker one night. When Larry lit my cigarette, someone inside the camp fired six rounds over our heads from an M-16, snatching the beret off my head. A friend of mine, a cadre leader in the FULRO, was poisoned to death in one of the villages, and another was beaten to death, with clubs, by a group of Vietnamese who ambushed him returning to his bunker after dark. Two hit men from Kontum followed me all over the camp during a camp celebration. I was drunk and kept drinking, while Nhual and FULRO bodyguards watched over me. After dark, the two hit men disappeared and were never seen again. FULRO men took them into the jungle, slit their throats, and dropped the bodies into the fast-moving Dak Poko River. Our agents discovered that the Vietnamese barber we hired, who gave me several haircuts, was also an assassin hired to kill me when the time was right. I threw a knife and clipped the top of his ear, threatened him, and had him carry a message to the Vietnamese. He ran onto a Caribou airplane before it departed Dak Pek and clung to a metal pipe in it, not letting anyone pull him off the aircraft.

The worst thing that happened, though, was the death of innocence. I had become very close with Plar, the little girl I wanted to adopt. The Vietnamese knew this, and one night she was grabbed, raped, and murdered, and her lifeless body was flung into the barbed wire on our perimeter. I started hating with a vengeance. I felt only Vietnamese blood could quench my thirst for revenge, but nothing could.

I drank even more, if that was possible. I also volunteered to take other team members' turns in leading operations out into the jungle. The main reason for this was to fight. I wanted to; I thirsted for it. I would sweat and ache and get dizzy, all for the sake of just a few minutes of heart-stopping, panic-stricken battle in which I could emerge shaken, nauseated, and scared to death but feeling victorious and invincible, with my negative thirst temporarily sated.

The other reason I spent most of my time in the jungle was that it was safer. The Vietnamese, our allies, were constantly trying to kill me in camp, where I was supposed to be safe. I was a warrior; the more I survived, the more I felt I couldn't be killed. I found this to be true with many in SF. There was an incredible, exaggerated sense of purpose.

When I was back and in the arms of my lover, Ning, I loved with as much passion as I fought. I don't mean violently, but quite the opposite. I made love with my whole body, mind, and being. When I entered the woman I loved,

I tried to melt into her body and become one, escaping the fears and horrors that were going on about me.

The strongest, toughest fighters I have ever seen were in Special Forces, but there was another common thread, and that was intelligence and a feeling of independence. The Vietnamese, North and South both, made war on children, and very few could understand that. Most of us believed that men maneuvered against each other and tried their best to kill each other, but Special Forces also believed in going into villages and teaching the people how to prevent bacteria and disease, grow crops, and improve their lot in life. In Vietnam, SF might go into a village one day and vaccinate all the children and return the next day to find all the children's left arms chopped off and piled in the middle of the village. That's one of the reasons Vietnam vets have Post Traumatic Stress Disorder.

I was a young man from Akron, Ohio, but Larry Vosen, from Cleveland, was even younger than I. Larry had worked at the C team in Pleiku and the B team in Kontum but was dying to get to an A camp and kick ass. Larry was eighteen years old when I first laid eyes on him. He looked like someone who had just earned a full football scholarship to Oklahoma or Notre Dame as an inside linebacker, and I couldn't figure out why in hell he was over in a hot little country shooting at people when he should be blitzing quarterbacks.

Larry was a nice guy, an E-5, and came into camp assigned as the light-weapons specialist, which he was learning in OJT. He also learned to be the backup engineer/demo man, receiving his training from Larry Crotsley. Larry Vosen got a lot of ribbing, however, over a little incident when Larry Crotsley was ready to go on R and R. One of Larry Crotsley's jobs was to destroy occasionally any unnecessary ordnance we had in the camp. He had a giant pit in the flat, down by the Dak Poko river due east of the camp. He would pile all the unexpended extra ordnance in the pit, set shape charges on top of it, facing down, and blow it with electric wire and detonator. Larry Crotsley asked Larry Vosen to gather up the surplus explosives around camp and destroy it, but he forgot to train him on that particular task. They piled several hundred pounds of different types of explosives on top of a number of boxes of TNT, which he wired with det cord attached to blasting caps and electric fuse.

When he blew the pitful of ordnance, artillery and mortar rounds, rockets, and other explosives flew into the air and rained down on the camp. The team commander—at the time, Capt. Mike Sizemore—was also away on R and R, and a large piece of shrapnel came through the roof of our team house and made a gaping hole through Sizemore's spot at the head of our long dining table.

An HE four-deuce mortar round fell through the roof of the LLDB team house, crashed through the second floor, and embedded itself in the concrete floor of the bottom level, right next to the LLDB team sergeant while the entire team was having a meeting.

Three four-deuce mortar rounds blew holes in the blacktop of our runway. One blew a large hole in the perimeter of our most eastern hill. One slightly wounded a Montagnard woman in the leg, but she was the only casualty.

Larry Vosen was well liked by the men on the team and was respected as well, and everyone knew that the accident wasn't really his fault. We were SF, however, so he was the brunt of some merciless ribbing for a couple of weeks.

It wasn't long after that that we experienced the "elephantburger incident," too.

A patrol was out on Bald Eagle Mountain, the tall lone peak at the southern end of the valley of the Dak Pek and the Dak Poko. The top had been cleared off by the 101st Airborne as a fire support base and was occupied; after that, by the 4th Division. The patrol was part of our recon platoon, made up of Montagnards only, our best fighters, and all were very dedicated members of the FULRO.

They camped near dusk on the top of the peak, and seven of the men didn't realize that they built their cooking fire on top of a buried 105-millimeter artillery round. The seven men had to be poured into body bags. Because we had been going through the monsoon season, it was very difficult to get air support. Commo Willy's boss, the senior radio operator, Sfc. Steve Olson, finally raised enough hell on the radio and a chopper came out, picked up the dead Montagnards, dropped their bodies off in front of the dispensary, and faded into the sunset, so to speak.

The patrol kept up their mission the next day, and on the northern side of the mountain, a little below where the jungle had been cleared out, they ran into a North Vietnamese resupply unit. The NVA were trying to carry supplies across one of the long ridges on the mountain by using an elephant.

I had a saying that I repeated many times in 'Nam: There were three men on a patrol who passed by a beautiful jungle flower. The first, an American, thought, What a beautiful flower: I'd like to give it to my mother. The second, a Vietnamese, thought, What a beautiful flower: I wonder what I can sell it to the American for? The third, a Montagnard, thought, I wonder what that tastes like?

It definitely describes the Central Highlands Vietnam experience.

When the NVA patrol passed by the hidden members from our recon platoon, the Yards decided it was time to recon by fire. Some of the NVA died and some ran away, but more important to the Dega was the dead elephant lying on the side of the mountain.

Because of a little lack of concern of men sitting behind desks in the bigger cities, and maybe partially because of difficulty in air transport, the men in my team at Dak Pek had been without meat for several weeks. We had eaten numerous cans of C rations and cans of pork and beans, but no fresh meat.

Sergeant Olson took a patrol up the mountain, and the elephant was butchered. The Yards packed the meat back down to the camp. At the camp we had a meat grinder.

Thanks to the Yards' hasty ambush, we ate elephantburgers for several weeks until our meat supply picked up again. To me, it was almost a delicacy anyway, as I spent most of my time out on operations eating LRRP rations. When back in camp, I almost always ate the normal fare of bats, rats, and monkeys in Yard villages, along with that smooth-but-potent rice wine.

In August 1968 I prepared to take one hundred of our strikers on an operation in the southeastern portion of our area of operations. Whenever we ran large operations, we always had two Americans and one or two LLDB, along with one interpreter and one hundred Yards. We tried to make sure we had one operation out like that at all times. Larry Vosen was the NCO who accompanied me on this particular operation. We operated in the valley of the Dak Poko, south of camp, between the North Vietnamese stronghold known as Tu Mrong Valley and the abandoned SF A camp of Dak Sut. In the case of this operation, we also had the LLDB team operations sergeant, who was a sergeant major and the LLDB heavy/light weapons specialist. Nhual was our interpreter.

By this time the FULRO had assigned six of the toughest, most experienced warriors we had as bodyguards. They shadowed me day and night and stayed close enough to rush in and intervene if the Vietnamese tried to kill me again. If I was killed the six bodyguards would be put to death for allowing it, but becoming my bodyguard was a very high status position among the Yards, second only to being an interpreter for our team.

I felt sorry for grunts in Army conventional units or the Marines when they went on operations "in the boonies." Most often they had to wear steel pots, flak jackets, giant packs with clothing, ammunition, grenades, and C rations. They were so loaded down with weight, they could hardly move.

I felt quite lucky to be in SF when it came to preparation for an operation. In SF, our motto was to travel light, so we didn't even carry shaving gear. Like each SF man, I had my own certain way of packing and particular things I carried on operations, but what I did and carried were somewhat normal for most A team members.

I wore one camouflaged "tiger suit" with the normal cargo pockets on the side and a large bamboo sheath sewn into the back of the right thigh, and in it, my giant Jeh knife, with the handle made of water buffalo horn and the brass inlaid, tooled, the blade made from the shrapnel of a five-hundred-pound bomb. In my left cargo pocket I carried my operations map, orders, notebook, grease pencil, and toothbrush. All of those were waterproofed with combat acetate. In my right cargo pocket I carried a pair of mosquito net gloves and a headnet I had purchased in a sporting goods store in the world. In my hip pocket I carried a hammock with a parachute suspension line attached to it. This was stretched tightly between two trees, with an Army poncho tied above it and anchored to form a canopy over me at night. In one of my cargo pockets I also carried a metal can holding a bottle of serum albumin blood expander IV solution. I had my wallet in my other hip pocket. In my left breast pocket I carried a taped-up package with five morphine Syrettes and extra matches and grease pencils. In the other breast pocket I carried a folded-up air signal panel as well as an Air Force survival signal mirror, which was also anchored to a string around my neck. In my right side pocket I carried cigarettes in a plastic container. I had a little pocket on my left sleeve in which I carried a plastic bottle of Army insect repellent for removing leeches. Around my neck I wore my dog tags, taped together to kill noise, and I had taped to them a miniature mirror, P-38 can opener, matches sealed in wax, and a fishhook and six-foot-line coiled up. This was my own E and E[9] survival kit, even if we got overrun while I was taking a shower.

I carried a small indigenous rucksack and took the plastic bags of dehydrated meals out of their plastic wrappers, taped them into small packs, and stuffed a week's worth into the bottom of the ruck. I carried one change of clean socks. I knew nobody who wore underwear in 'Nam —it was always too hot and humid. I carried a whetstone, cleaning patches, and solvent for my weapon, toilet paper, soap, coffee, tea, and cocoa. I also carried my poncho and

9. Escape and evasion.

poncho liner and as much extra ammunition and grenades as I could carry. In the pouches on the outside of the ruck I carried extra canteens of water, a bottle of salt pills, and a bottle of tetracycline. I was allergic to penicillin and the bite of a common bug in the jungle we called a bloodfly. I got bitten by them a lot and my face or hand would swell several times its normal size, so I would swallow a whole bottle of tetracycline if bitten by one. I also had a two-quart bladder canteen lashed onto the pack.

Instead of a normal Army ammo belt, I wore a World War II–vintage BAR belt and harness. It contained four pouches, and I kept three loaded magazines in each, upside down, to keep dirt out, and a fourth sideways on top of the other three under the flap. In case of a firefight, I could eject a spent magazine, toss it into the open neck of my shirt, and quickly grab and load another from the BAR belt. Each magazine held twenty rounds, but I only used eighteen, as the early M-16 magazines had weak springs. I also loaded a tracer as the thirteenth round and used tracers for the sixteenth, seventeenth, and eighteenth. This let me know when I was at the end of a magazine.

On the harness I wore another knife, a Ka-Bar taped upside down, two HE hand grenades, and two smoke grenades. On the front of the belt I had an Army bandage. In case of emergency or capture, I had a large switchblade knife taped to my right calf. On some operations, when I expected confronting numerous bunkers or Soviet-made tanks, I also carried an M-72 LAW portable, expendable rocket launcher strapped across the top of my indigenous pack.

My rifle, the CAR-15, was ideal for jungle fighting. It differed from its bigger brother, the M-16, in three ways: One, the barrel was sawed off. Two, the front stock was round and ribbed, whereas the M-16's was triangularly shaped. Three, the rear stock was a tube with a squeeze-type stock over it that telescoped back.

I wore a camouflaged cowboy hat on my head and a black cowboy kerchief around my neck. Under my tiger suit jacket I wore a dark green jungle sweater, warm on cold nights and cooling in the hot sun.

Like many SFers, I carried one more thing, which I considered a necessity: a garrote. Made of piano wire, it was about eighteen inches long, with wooden handles on each end. If you had to take out a sentry or kill someone silently, you crossed the ends of the wire and your hands and slipped the loop over your victim's head. You quickly tightened the loop, then twisted, lifting him onto your back while you pulled hard on both handles. The piano wire would pass through the windpipe and neck muscles and finally between the disks in the vertebrae, slicing the person's head off.

The night before we left on the operation was tense, as it always was, between Ning and me. We had fought, because she was afraid every time I went out into the jungle. It was an ongoing thing, however, because I seemed to spend most all of my time on operations. I loved it in the jungle chasing those emotional highs.

When in camp, higher headquarters wanted us to turn in volumes of paperwork, and I was the worst in the team in getting my mine prepared. If someone told me that I had to prepare some kind of report, I asked him to do it for me.

I would grin and say, "Just use a bunch of big words, abbreviate as much as possible, punctuate as little as possible, and they'll never know the difference as long as you submit it in triplicate."

Ning was lying in my bed when I walked into the bunker right after dark. I carried a makeshift tray with two plates. There were two baked potatoes, salads, elephant steaks, and glasses of wine. In the middle of the tray I placed a glass-size metal can that serum albumin was packed in. It was half filled with water, and I had placed an arrangement of pink, purple, and white jungle flowers in it.

Ning smiled, flipping the blanket and sheet off, revealing her very curvaceous body. She stood up and wrapped the sheet around herself like a sarong. We sat on the edge of the bed and ate our meals. Ning stuck a pink flower through her hair over her right ear. I kept trying to eat, but she set her plate down and started removing my clothing. I lost my appetite for food. I was soon naked, looking for a place to set my plate down. Ning got on her knees in front of me and smiled impishly up into my eyes.

"Look," she said, pointing to my groin, "you spill your food. I clean up."

An hour later, we lay in bed, Ning's body covered with flower petals. Her head was on my chest, and I slowly stroked her long, shiny, black hair. I felt like Charlie could kill me then, and it would be okay.

I rolled over and looked down into her black eyes. They smiled up at me, and we kissed softly and long.

"What about you, me?" she asked softly.

"My wife and I wrote about getting a divorce," I said. "I have put in for my extension to stay in 'Nam. You and I can get married, and I will stay here until the war's over, then stay and fight for your people's rights."

"What about go America?" she asked innocently.

"After we have many babies, and I fight for your independence. Do you want to live there?"

"No," she replied, her eyes opening wide, "I *beaucoup*

scared. No have school, not smart. You fall in love with beautiful American girl with yellow hair."

I chuckled. "No, Ning, I'm in love with stupid Montagnard girl."

We both giggled and kissed again. I picked up a flower petal with my lips and flicked it across her nipples, stomach, and everywhere I thought would make her moan and purr.

I slid up and looked down into her eyes again. They got very serious, and I stroked her hair, knowing she was troubled and going to say something important.

"What if you die?" she asked.

I started to answer, but she continued, "Or maybe same-same, maybe you get shot or *beaucoup* sick? They send you home America?"

I thought for a minute and said, "Ning, I do not know what will happen each day. I only know that you and I are survivors. No matter what happens to either one of us, we will both survive. You must always think that way. I also know that they cannot kill me."

She smiled, and in a simple but profound Montagnard statement shook me to the core by saying, "Don, you are a man. You are not Jesus."

"No, I'm not," I replied, "but God has spoken to me with his actions. He has protected me so many times from assassination attempts, I just feel He won't let me die."

Ning's eyes clouded with tears.

"Maybe sometimes people love you die same-same."

I pictured little Plar's half-nude bloody body in the barbed wire. Tears formed in my eyes, and I held Ning tightly. She cried. The macho facade of those, my youthful days, wouldn't allow her to hear my silent sobs. I'm sure her cheeks felt the moistness in the pillow afterward, though.

"Ning," I said after a few minutes, "I can only tell you this: I love you with all my heart, and we only have today. If we are alive and together tomorrow, we will have that day, too, but today we have each other."

Our bodies melted together in a long, passionate kiss, and we made love long into the night.

The sun peeked up over the mountains by Tu Mrong Valley, and the early-morning rays pierced slits through the veil of fog hovering over the valley of the Dak Poko. The last men in my column crossed the makeshift footbridge over the deep Dak Pek River, and we wound our way past the most southern villages in the valley, headed along the base of Bald Eagle Mountain. The skies were still socked in bad by monsoons, so we would have to hump it to our AO.[10]

Nguyen Van Dong grew up in Saigon. He was drafted into the ARVN and spent one year getting shot at by VC and NVA. He didn't like that at all, so on one pass into Saigon Dong borrowed some civilian clothes from an old neighborhood buddy and got away fast. One month later, he found himself bumming around the bars in Kontum, where he was living at his cousin's house—the cousin who was a member of the LLDB team at Dak Pek.

There were too many questions asked in Saigon, as he was in his early twenties and not serving in the Army or working at a job. He was questioned several times as a possible VC and also was questioned about a bar robbery.

He moved to Dak Pek, where he was immediately put on the private payroll as a spy. He was told to romance a

10. Area of operations.

rather attractive Montagnard woman who seemed to be a status seeker. He was to act like he was a reformer and was sympathetic to the plight of the Dega and use the woman, named Triu, to get intelligence on the activities of the FULRO in and around Dak Pek.

Dong started romancing Triu and spent money on her, which which the Vietnamese gladly supplied him. She loved the presents and courtship, but she was the only Montagnard who was fooled. Our spies treated him nicely, welcoming him into the fold, so to speak, while keeping all eyes and ears on him.

They only saw each other for a short period of time, and he went to her distraught parents with a pig, several chickens, and a bag of rice—a high price to pay for a be-trothal, but even so, her father reportedly spit in Dong's face. The next day, a little boy, Triu's cousin, was found floating facedown in the Dak Poko. He had been tortured. Dong and Triu got married not long after.

Dong did find out some information about the FULRO, by simply drinking rice wine with some loose-lipped Yards. It was believed he fingered several FULRO cadre members who were assassinated by the Vietnamese. Some of the leadership decided he needed to be elimi-nated. Dong was on the operation with us and didn't know he was a marked man.

We crossed over the Dak Poko and traveled along its eastern bank, arriving by midafternoon at the northern end of our AO, where we set up a perimeter for the night.

The second day, due east of the ruins of Dak Sut, our point patrol opened fire for several seconds. We halted the column, and the front men moved forward quickly. They signaled the forward element to halt the column. I was summoned forward with Nhual, accompanied by the LLDB weapons sergeant.

Nhual whispered, "If we get into fight with NVA, Dong will take many bullets in the back."

I winked at my friend, and we met up with the point. *"My wa huh?"* I asked.

The men spoke excitedly, and curious, I moved forward with them, Nhual, and the LLVC. In the middle of the trail was a half-eaten wild pig, its bloody entrails pulled out. One of the Yards, wide-eyed, pointed at several saucer-size tracks in the dark, muddy trail. It was a tiger—a big one.

Nhual said, "Trung-uy, they walked around that bend in the trail, and the tiger was eating the pig's stomach. It growled at them, but ran fast when they shot at it."

I lit a Lucky Strike and looked at the large tracks again.

"Ba Nua," I said, using the name I usually called Nhual and that meant "father of Nua," "Do you think that might be the tiger that's eaten several villagers?"

"Yes, not too many tigers live in area around the camp. They have AO just like us."

I grinned, thinking about the simple but clever comparison.

The next day, in the southeastern sector of the AO, we sent numerous squad-size patrols out to look for signs of enemy troop movements. Prior to the operation, I had flown out on VR[11] with a helicopter and spotted a squad of VC carrying baskets of mountain rice through this same area. I pulled out three HE hand grenades and had the chopper fly back directly over the VC as they tried to flee

11. Visual reconnaissance.

into the jungle, and I threw the grenades down on them. We took ground fire, but most of them were too busy looking for a big brass bed to hide under to shoot.

That night, as usual, I had the men dig in night positions, waited until dark, then moved to our real positions. I pulled my little nylon hammock out of my pocket, stretched the parachute suspension lines and tied them tightly between two trees, then made a canopy above the hammock with my dark green poncho. I stuck a forked stick in the ground and hung my CAR-15 and ammo belt on a harness on it. In front of the bigger stick I stuck two smaller ones and placed my jungle boots upside down on them. This not only allowed them and my feet to dry out but also kept nasty critters from crawling in during the night. It would be most inconvenient to get hit during the night, yank my boots on, and get bitten by one of the many deadly bugs or snakes in the jungle. I pulled on my mosquito mittens and headnet and went to sleep.

The noise was like an attacking bowling alley on league night. I jumped out of my hammock, reached for the CAR-15 and harness, and grabbed my jungle boots. I still had my mosquito mittens and headnet on, which I quickly shed, and my mind was racing through a subconscious checklist of potential dangers. Nothing registered.

I heard Montagnards, above the rumbling noise, chattering unintelligibly, but I could tell they were still in their positions. No shots had been fired, but the noise was getting louder. The night was so black and the jungle so thick, I couldn't even see my hand in front of my face. Whatever was making the noise was coming through the underbrush right across our perimeter, and there was a lot of grunting, trampling of sticks, leaves, and tearing of vines and branches. I heard the invisible cloud of havoc approach and pass directly below and around me. There was more murmuring and yelling by the Yards as the noise passed on downhill from us and soon died out. The next morning we discovered it had been a herd of wild pigs.

The first week of the operation was pretty much uneventful as operations went, but a major problem came up at the end of that period. My Yards and I carried a week's worth of food in our rucksacks out in the field, and we got another week's worth the day before the food ran out. Monsoons were racking the Central Highlands, however, and all air support was at a standstill. Because of this, I called for resupply a day early; however, nothing but a sharp instrument could penetrate the thick cloud cover. The overcast was so thick, I bet that five-hundred-pound bombs dropped from B-52's bounced back up in the air off the top of the clouds.

Two days later, I was out of food and so were my Yards. It was simple: food one day and none the next. At the time, personally worse for me was the fact that I had no cigarettes either.

This was a big deal with me. We couldn't get choppers, and I was upset, but it didn't seem even to faze the Montagnards. When mealtime came, cooking fires were built all around our perimeter and small groups of strikers came in from self-appointed patrols in the jungle. They carried various types of roots, grasses, and small animals to their fires. Others sitting around the small piles of flaming sticks quickly prepared various types of meals. Several Dega came to a fire one of my bodyguards prepared and quickly started roasting several small rodents, which had already been dressed out.

I did not like to have the two Americans close to each other preparing or staying in night positions. One grenade, mortar, or rocket could wipe us both out. In case we got overrun during the night, we could each take half of the command and run things, too. Rendezvous points in case of such an attack were discussed every time we stopped. I assumed Larry Vosen, on the other side of our perimeter, was being treated to a meal similar to mine. He was. In fact, we both were fed meals from the jungle for the next five days. One of the LLDB on the operation had Vietnamese cigarettes with him, so I paid him an arm and a leg for them and smoked them. It was almost as much fun as smoking rat tails.

During this time, Chuck Challela, who was formerly the light-weapons NCO at Dak Pek, had gotten into a big shoot-out at his new camp, Dak Seang. Dak Seang, our sister camp to the south, had been hit by a regiment of NVA, with many sappers breaching the barbed wire. The first night, Chuck and the team commander, Capt. Jimmy Chiles, each earned themselves Silver Stars, which would have been Distinguished Service Crosses had they been in a conventional unit. The two scrambled around the camp perimeter under fire, fortifying, resupplying, and motivating all their positions, and Chuck even crawled up in a machine-gun tower and did some shooting. That doesn't mean the rest of the team was holed in their bunkers watching television. The team, incredibly, repelled the attack, leaving the bodies of numerous NVA suicide sappers in the barbed wire.

After the initial assault, the NVA kept Dak Seang under siege for days, mortaring any aircraft that attempted to land. C-7A Caribous had to fly over the camp and air-drop supplies by parachute when the planes could get in the air.

The 4th Infantry Division combat-assaulted a battalion of grunts onto the deserted fire support bases in the range due west of the camp, and they had to be extracted immediately. The NVA occupied those hills and the shorter foothills closer to camp, moving their mortars around from spot to spot and taking refuge in deep bunkers dug into the steep slopes on various ridgelines. They also dug in numerous antiaircraft positions all along the edges of the mountain ridges. They fired at aircraft coming near the camp, then moved their big guns to a different position before air strikes came in and rained ordnance on their location.

During this period, a 4th Division dust-off, or medevac helicopter, was shot down on one of the ridges due southwest of the camp. The crew and even wounded escaped under fire and made it all the way back to Dak Seang; however, the dust-off pilot was shot through the legs and immediately surrounded and captured by swarms of NVA from the tough 24th Regiment of the 2d Division.

While we were going through the fourth day of trying to figure out what little creature we were eating for breakfast, lunch, and supper, Chuck Challela got into a firefight with a bunch of NVA punks outside his camp. Fortunately, he had about one hundred Jeh, Sedang, and Halang Yards with him, and they kicked ass, losing a few in the process, but the NVA lost more.

I called Dak Seang and asked them if they'd like some help. They said they'd love it, and my team commander approved it, so we headed for the wide and swift-running Dak Poko River. Dak Seang sent a squad-size patrol, carrying ropes, to the river, so we could make a crossing.

We met them just above a major bend in the white water due east of Dak Seang. We halted on the bank of the watercourse, put out flankers and a rear guard, and waited. After half an hour, the Yards suddenly got very quiet and cocked their weapons. This happened quite often. They just seemed to sense when danger was upon us. An NVA appeared on the far bank. One second he wasn't there, and the next second he was. He stared across the river and tried to spot us. He held an AK-47 at the ready, was dressed in a khaki uniform, and wore a tan pith helmet with a red star in the center.

I flipped the lever on my CAR-15 to automatic and put the front bead on the center of his chest. He looked all around, but our men were well hidden. My Yards were disciplined and knew to wait until I fired first. My finger started to squeeze slightly on the trigger, but I held off, waiting to see how many more NVA would show up. He wasn't a trail watcher, as he would probably not be carrying a fairly good AK and wearing a good uniform, and there were no major trails close to that spot in the river. He looked into the jungle behind him and signaled some un-seen cohorts forward with a large sweep of his arm.

Seconds later, a squad of Jeh strikers appeared in ti-ger suits and carrying carbines. They were clearly from Dak Seang. We all jumped up, waving and yelling at them. They laughed and yelled back, and I breathed a sigh of relief.

Some Special Forces people outfitted their point men with NVA uniforms and weapons to throw off the point men or ambushes they might wander into by mistake. I sometimes had my point men wear loincloths for the same reason, to throw off the NVA patrols and buy us an extra few seconds to attack first and not get caught in a bad position.

The Dak Seang squad produced a small rope that was tied to a rifle grenade attached to an M-1 carbine, but the pin hadn't been pulled. The NVA-garbed point man lifted the M-1, aimed it at me, and fired. Larry Vosen had moved up next to me, and we watched the grenade fly across the angry waters, trailing something behind it. It landed with a thunk right between us. We looked down at the un-detonated grenade with a nylon line tied to it, then looked up at each other and grinned, realizing how stupid we had been letting a rifle grenade land at our feet. The only thing separating us from sure death was a cotter pin.

Larry and two Yards grabbed the nylon line and pulled it across the river. It was tied, with a blood knot, to another line much larger in circumference, and the end of it was wrapped around a large tree and tied off about eight feet above the ground. A Yard on the other side of the river did the same thing over there.

One of the CIDG stripped off his weapon, ammo harness, and rucksack, and volunteered to go across first. The rope was nylon, so it stretched, and when he grabbed it and went down the bank, it went into the river and the man had to go hand over hand.

My oldest son is close to being an Olympic-level white-water kayaker and "boats" some of the most ferocious white water in North America, all over the western United States. The Dak Poko could qualify for the list, especially when it was swollen with rushing water from the monsoons at that time. There was one thing even more treacherous about the Dak Poko, however, and that was the myriad of vines, sunken trunks, roots, and tangles. On top of that, most U.S. kayakers and rafters don't expose themselves to enemy fire.

The first Yard made it across okay and so did the second. Men were actually cheering on both banks as they made it across, but neither man carried a weapon or a pack.

Nhual looked at the assembled strikers, and speaking in Jeh said, "The next man needs to carry his weapons across."

I looked directly at Dong, our Vietnamese spy married to the Montagnard. He spoke Jeh fluently and understood Nhual's words. His eyes searched for a place to hide, so I grinned at him to put him on the spot even more. The two LLDB sergeants stood near me, so Dong, apparently wanting to impress them and probably feeling pressured by my constant gaze, gave a slight wave and said he would go next. I turned, giving Nhual a grin and a wink.

Dong grabbed the rope and stood next to the churning water. He watched the millions of gallons rushing by and gulped as he looked all the way across at the far bank. The Dak Seang strikers across the river cheered as they saw him enter the water after slinging his rifle and the other two across his back. They only saw a striker in a tiger suit braving the waters, but at that distance couldn't tell it was a Vietnamese.

I watched Dong as he started hand over hand across the rope, the river stretching way out and his body being tugged and pulled out as he was stretched out twenty feet downstream from us. I remembered one day at infantry OCS when we were out in the field and had several classes on river crossings. It was the coldest day of the winter at Fort Benning, Georgia, and we all had to remove all our clothing on the banks of the Chattahoochee River. We folded our ponchos into rectangles and filled them with dry pine needles and our clothing. Then we folded the side and ends over and tied them all into personal-size dark green rafts. We each placed our weapons on the little expedient rafts and folded our arms across them and then kicked across the fast-rushing rapids with strict orders from the

TAC officer not to let our weapons get wet. He didn't care if we drowned as long as the weapons stayed dry. On the other side we had one man swim across the river with a line and tie it off while we donned our clothing and equipment, and we crossed back across the river, wearing our clothing this time. I still remember how much drag there was and how tired my arms and legs got.

I knew that Dong wasn't going to make it. Three quarters of the way across, one of the rapids boiled up over his head and only his arms were visible as he struggled to keep crossing one hand over the other and pulling across the line. He made it about five more feet, and by that time his head had been submerged under a steady flow of rushing water for several minutes. I glanced at Nhual and several FULRO cadre members, and they all gave me slight nods and grins. There was movement next to me, and I saw Larry Vosen stripping his boots off; God bless heroes.

I grabbed his arm and said, "No, Sergeant Vosen, I have too many men who need you here, with us. The other side's closer."

As I spoke, I saw two Dak Seang strikers stripping off their uniforms and boots. Dong's arms came off the rope and went straight up in the air, and he sank under the churning water. The two Yards dived in and swam downstream. A few minutes later his head and shoulders came up and bobbed once, then went back under. The weapons and rucksack were gone from his shoulders.

One of the Dak Seang Yards went under with a whale roll and came up with Dong's head under his arm. He backstroked with his free arm toward the shore, and two more strikers extended a quickly cut length of bamboo to him. He grabbed the end, and they pulled him to the steep bank. He finally turned his head and looked at Dong's face and saw that he was Vietnamese and shoved Dong's head back underwater and climbed out.

Speaking in Jeh, he yelled, "He's already dead!"

"Choi oi! Choi doc oi!" the LLVC team sergeant raged.

I said softly, *"Xin loi, Trung-si."*

I turned toward Nhual and the other FULRO leaders and did everything I could to keep from breaking out in uproarious laughter. They snickered, too, like schoolkids, and stopped as the other LLDB turned, hearing the noises. Everyone looked somber until he turned around once more.

Larry Vosen stepped over and said, "I want to go next, sir. It'll be a good example for the Yards."

"Thanks, Sergeant Vosen, but we will wait for aircraft to take us."

He didn't like that. He was excited and wanted action, and I knew and understood the feeling, but I was still the commander and responsible for one hundred lives. I knew that Larry, many others, and I could make it across easily, but I also knew that some, especially some of the older men with us, wouldn't make it and would meet the same fate as Dong. That wasn't going to happen. I didn't explain my decision, which I still don't like doing. We waited for the sky to clear, and I directed our other two men to accompany the Dak Seang patrol back to their camp.

Larry was pissed, so I let him be pissed. To me, sometimes you can gauge your performance as a military commander by whether your men are angry. Sometimes, if they are not angry, you are not making the tough decisions.

The next day, choppers came in, picked up my men, and hauled us across the Dak Poko. We went through the jungle a short distance and made it into the besieged camp of Dak Seang during a mortar concentration. They also brought in a company from the A camp of Mang Buk and another company from our B team Mike force[12] in Kontum.

That is when I first met Capt. Joseph K. Dietrich. Sfc. Steve Owens from Dak Pek described Joe Dietrich best when he said that he looked like a miniature version of Arnold Schwarzenegger with a flattop and glasses. Joe was the commander of the Mike force and had been CO of the A team at Plei Me and also liaison to the 4th Infantry Division at Pleiku. I cannot tell about him here, because the story is too long and too interesting, so I will just give you a preview.

Each unit was going to cover a certain area of operations West of Dak Seang on a search-and-destroy mission. The B team executive officer was going to be the overall commander, except he was only there for the briefing, and Joe Dietrich actually was in charge. Joe's company was to sweep due west of the camp and take over an enemy-occupied fire support base overlooking the camp. The force from Mang Buk was to sweep southwest of the camp, paralleling the Mike force, and my unit, along with reinforcements from Dak Seang and Chuck Challela, was to sweep southwest from the camp. I also was given the additional mission of locating the captured medevac pilot, if possible, and free him, or recover his body if he was dead. Also, we were to locate the downed medevac helicopter and destroy it so the NVA couldn't salvage anything from it.

Dak Seang had a pet monkey, and several of the guys had been dipping into the sauce, along with Joe Dietrich

12. Mobile strike force.

and his Mike force NCOs. The B team XO was sitting in Bermuda shorts and a baseball cap behind the team house sunning himself, so Dietrich and the others decided to have some fun. The XO had been transferred into the 5th Group from the 1st Cav because of an apparent shortage of field-grade officers, as he was totally unqualified for Special Forces. In fact, he wasn't even airborne: He was a "leg." However, he wore an unauthorized full flash on his beret, and this griped the hell out of anybody and everybody who knew about it. Green berets, jumpwings, and full-flash qualifications were things that not everybody legitimately had, and there was a lot of professional pride in them. Consequently, someone wearing one of them who hadn't earned it really pissed some people off.

As a joke, Dietrich started teasing the Dak Seang team members about them having a monkey who was their mascot, and he wasn't even airborne-qualified. They picked up on the joking and joked right back about it. This was all done to infuriate the XO, who sat there, the whole time, listening in on the conversation. Someone took a parachute flare apart and made a parachute harness for the monkey. They attached it to the parachute from the flare and dropped the monkey off the machine gun tower five times to make him airborne. Many jokes were made about the monkey being airborne and how imperative it was for anyone connected to SF. The major left the camp not long after.

In fact, I was kind of happy when he left, as I started having radio trouble. The jungle had been cleared away from the camp for some distance, so it was a fairly flat field of thick tanglefoot and overgrown mountain rice fields out to the edge of the jungle. When my operation left the camp, heading across the open area, we started taking two incoming 82-millimeter mortar rounds every five minutes for an hour. Hearing the hollow "thunk" sounds of the mortars leaving the tube, knowing that they are aimed at you, and waiting for them to hit were some of the longest, scariest, most nerve-racking minutes in my life.

After that, our point got hit, and we had one hell of a rerun of the Shoot-out at the OK Corral. I lost some good men in that firefight, including my favorite bodyguard, a father of five who took a bunch of lead meant for me. Chuck Challela and Larry Vosen both performed very well and bravely. It was Larry's first time under fire, and he was definitely SF. I also had a parachute flare blow up while I fired it for a FAC[13] flying overhead who put in air strikes for me. My right wrist was messed up and wrapped with pressure bandages, and I had to fire and do everything left-handed.

Unfortunately, there was another young E-5 with us from Dak Seang, whom I relieved for cowardice after the street fight. During the fight, I almost blew his head off for arguing in combat with Chuck Challela. At a time like that, you have to take swift, stern measures or men will panic, do the wrong things, and get themselves and others killed. I threatened to shoot the man with my gun barrel pointed at his tonsils, and I was not bluffing. Even in SF there were occasionally bad apples, but not often.

After we chased the NVA off toward Laos, we set out southwest and uphill to locate the dust-off pilot and chopper. On the way, I got into an argument over the radio with the XO, again seated on his lawn chair back at Dak Seang. He picked out a spot on the map, which he directed me to go to. Unfortunately, the team sergeant from Dak Pek was

13. Forward air controller.

the actual commander of the operation and I was just his X ray, his adviser. I explained this to the XO, but he didn't care and was soon barking orders at me about forcing the company to go where he said. I asked if he wanted me to take them at gunpoint, and he said he didn't care as long as I did what he said. I again explained that the USSF cannot order the VNSF what to do, as we were the advisers, technically subservient to them. No argument worked, so I suddenly developed radio trouble, told him I couldn't hear him, and threw the radio's mike on the ground.

Another factor entering into that decision was the fact that the LLVC team sergeant and I argued about where we were located. He pointed to one spot on the map and I, another, about two clicks (kilometers) away. We picked out a sharp peak on the end of a steep ridge and agreed it was a distinguishable terrain feature on the map and on the ground. On top of that, we bet each other two cases of American beer. I knew I was right and was dying to win, just to make the old Trung-si lose face. We measured how far we went from tree to tree and shot azimuths on the peak. Arriving there later in the day, we sat down and looked across the valley, and he had to admit to me that I was right and he was wrong. Even in the Vietnam War there were some days that I was just happy I had awakened for.

Heading toward the peak, we crossed a major trail intersection in the jungle and heard several spaced shots from an AK-47. I checked to find out when my last man was clearly past the intersection, and I called for our hourly smoke break. Every fifty minutes I gave the men a halt and they had a cigarette, burned leeches off their legs and necks, drank water, and ate salt pills.

I called Dak Seang on the PRC-25 while Larry Vosen

and Chuck Challela sat on the muddy trail and talked between canteen sips.

"What's Lieutenant Bendell doing?" Larry asked.

Chuck grinned and said, "You hear that familiar old tinny sound of an AK being fired a while back?"

"Yeah, I did hear that," Larry answered.

Chuck continued, "The NVA put trail watchers at every major trail intersection. After we passed, he fired three spaced shots, indicating that we were a company-size unit. Then the little yellow fucker fired one shot, which let his boss know what our direction of travel is. I suppose ole Clint Eastwood there is calling in artillery on the fuck right now and is going to blow his little yellow balls off."

Both men laughed, and Chuck took a long, slow drag on his cigarette. I joined the two men, my Yard RTO[14] following me. I lit up and started burning leeches off my legs.

I said, "I just called Dak Seang and asked for a one-o-five concentration on that trail watcher back there. You guys heard 'em?"

They both nodded and I went on, "They already have the trail junction plotted, so we're going to try a concentration instead of spotting rounds first."

Chuck asked, "What about the triple-canopy jungle, Trung-uy? The rounds'll go off before they break through it all."

I said, "I called for VT[15] fuses. They'll blow up before they hit the ground and give an air-burst effect."

Larry gave Chuck a questioning look, and Chuck said, "He called for rounds you normally use on bunkers. When

14. The guy who carries the radio.
15. Variable timing.

they first hit, they don't go off for a second or so. They'll hit the canopy, punch through, and blow up before they hit the ground."

We heard far-off booming sounds, and a voice came over the radio, *"Dan lua, cuoi cung."*

I replied, *"Da u, cuoi cung."*

Larry gave Chuck another questioning look, and Chuck explained, "The LLDB are manning the howitzers, so he called it in to them in Vietnamese. They probably think he's one of them."

Larry laughed, and a split second later, the jungle was shattered by tremendous explosions behind us. I had Chuck and Larry set up hasty ambush positions and took a squad-size patrol back myself for the BDA.[16] We found pieces of the trail watcher all over the place, in trees, bushes, and scattered around.

An hour later, after some more skirmishes with the now fleeing NVA, we made it to the medevac helicopter. The NVA had stripped it of everything usable. After that, we found the pilot, or at least his remains. The Geneva Convention was a joke to the NVA. The pilot was originally wounded through the thighs, but Ho Chi's boys weren't satisfied with that. They broke every joint in his body and shot him through the forehead with an AK, blowing the back of his skull off. They left him lying there for us on his own stretcher. We had to fold him into a body bag.

I looked forward to our return to Dak Pek, as we had been out in the jungle on a continuous operation for almost a month straight. Larry and I had not shaved, bathed, showered, or changed clothes. We didn't need insect repellent—the mosquitoes bounced off our smell.

16. Bomb damage assessment.

The following day I went out with another squad-size patrol just for the emotional high. We ran into a couple of NVA, who scrambled into a tunnel. Well, here was Bendell's chance to overcome his fear after the tunnel incident in Camp A. P. Hill, Virginia. I got a U.S. Army Colt .45 automatic from the LLDB weapons sergeant who went with us, and one of the Yards supplied me with a flashlight. The tunnel entrance was dug right into the side of a B-52 bomb crater on the eastern side of the mountain toward Dak Seang.

I gave Nhual a nervous look and crawled, headfirst, into the tiny black hole. It would have taken a sledge-hammer—no, a jackhammer—to pound a straightpin into my rectum right then.

The dull flashlight beam showed me the tunnel went into the mountain and slanted down and turned toward the right. My wrist was still hurt and sore, so I had to half-carry the flashlight by pressing it against my chest. I gulped and crawled forward. Suddenly, blackness, and I couldn't breathe. The tunnel had caved in, but you know what? I wasn't the least bit scared. I held my breath and pinched my nostrils together. The feeling was crushing, and it would have been nearly impossible to expand my chest anyway. For some reason, I felt such a security with the Yards with me, there was simply a confidence that they would not let me die. I was right; I felt several sets of hands grabbing my calves and lower legs. Next, I felt hands desperately clawing dirt off of my back and rear, while the rest pulled me backward.

In seconds I was blinking that hot Vietnam sun out of my eyes. I am convinced that God controls the sun that rises and sets over the state of Colorado, but the one over Vietnam is a different sun, which God lets Satan control.

In fact, I believe that the devil turned the thermostat up on it every time I went out on operations.

I sat up shaking dirt out of my clothes, and I started laughing. Soon the Yards joined in, and we laughed like a bunch of crazy fools, or maybe just very frightened ones. I drank a quart of water and swallowed two salt pills, then lit up a little cigarillo.

Grinning at Nhual, I said, "If I ever again tell you that I'm going to crawl headfirst into a tunnel, be my friend and make sure it has pubic hair around it."

I chuckled at my own joke and Nhual politely did as well, but he said, "What is pubic hair?"

I fell over sideways laughing. It was time to go home to Dak Pek.

4

Joe Dietrich

When I returned to Dak Pek, Capt. Joe Dietrich of the Mike force came there as well, as the new team commander. Joe was not an average guy or an average commander. He was short, but he was a man, and he was SF. About five feet seven, he had a flattop haircut, wore glasses, and obviously lifted weights. He also wore a Smith & Wesson .41 magnum revolver in a black quick-draw holster, an involuntary gift from a Viet Cong regimental commander. He spoke with just a hint of his native German accent. Joe and an aunt escaped from East Germany when he was a child, and he eventually made it to America with all kinds of childhood memories, like being fired on by Soviet tanks.

When Joe first came to II Corps, he was assigned as the A-team CO at Plei Me, but that's a different story in itself; so was his short-lived job as liaison to the 4th Infantry Division, headquartered in Pleiku. Following that, he became CO of the B-24 Mike force at Kontum, and finally the CO at Dak Pek. Joe had a way of making waves very quietly and often humorously.

He also had a reputation of being unsafe, or very, very gung ho, at best. Joe took notes constantly. Being a good SF officer, he kept a CYA[1] file and notebooks. This, too,

1. Cover your ass.

made incompetent commanders nervous. It's funny, but a person taking notes all the time is applauded by a good manager and feared by a bad one. Joe's biggest rep, though, came from his jeep-driving.

On Highway 14 between Pleiku and Kontum, convoys constantly got ambushed by NVA and VC day and night. There were numerous rocket and mortar attacks, and the road was mined daily by the NVA and VC. The most common place where the attacks occurred was a lonely strip between the two cities, paralleled by a big jungle-covered mountain due west of the road. In fact, it was called VC Mountain, and Joe tested its evil spirits constantly.

One night (that's right, night; Joe drove the road all the time after dark, even though it was off-limits), Joe roared down the darkened road, with no lights on his jeep, navigating only by the moonlight. He came to a wide curve and was not aware that an air strike had been called in earlier. There was a twenty-foot-wide and fifteen-foot-deep five-hundred-pound bomb crater on the edge of the highway, right where the road curved sharply to the left for southbound vehicles. Joe was on his way to Pleiku and went flying over the lip of the crater in his speeding jeep. In actuality, it was an Army Willys one-quarter-ton truck, but everyone called it a jeep.

Joe shook his head and looked around. He saw nothing but the walls of a bomb crater. Far off, he heard the rumble of an Arc Light, a B-52 carpet bomb strike. Joe pulled the .41 magnum out of the left side of his waistband, the place he carried it whenever he drove the jeep, and replaced it in the holster on his right hip. He also had a Swedish K slung around his neck, and he jacked a round in a chamber, flipping the selector on safe. Dietrich crawled up the edge of the bomb crater and peeked out into the darkness. He couldn't make out anything in the shadow of the not-too-distant mountain, but he heard voices far off, and the language was Vietnamese. He didn't want to stick around and practice intelligence analysis on the voices, nor did he want to play John Wayne. Captain Dietrich wanted to put his immediate past behind him. He wanted any big holes in the ground visible only in his rearview mirror.

Joe scrambled and tumbled back down to the jeep, started it up, and went for it. He rocked it back and forth in four-wheel drive and gunned it up over the edge of the crater. It was so steep driving up out of the deep hole, he felt like it was going to tumble over backward, but the vehicle roared up and over and into the night sky. Joe switched to high-range two-wheel drive and booked it for Pleiku, thanking God he wasn't headed toward Kontum.

In Kontum, the QCs—the Vietnamese "white mice" MPs—set up roadblocks on random streets throughout the city. Several nights, Joe roared into Kontum, lights out, rounded a corner, and took shots from a VN roadblock. He would jam it in reverse and skid back around the corner, seeking a safer route to the B-24 or Mike force compounds.

He made it to Pleiku without further problems, but two weeks later, Captain Dietrich had to make it to Kontum for a meeting. It was daytime, but Joe couldn't hop on any aircraft, so he borrowed a jeep from Pleiku Mike force. He bluffed his way by the MP roadblocks outside Pleiku and took off down the busy peasant-covered highway at top speed. Joe saw explosions and smoke ahead of him when he was about halfway between the two cities. Off to his left stood the quiet but deadly VC Mountain. Suddenly he saw the distant view of an F-4A Phantom jet seemingly shooting up out of the ground ahead of him. As it climbed up through the cloud cover at ten grand, Joe heard the distant explosion of a five-hundred-pounder and saw a black cloud of smoke billowing up from the horizon. Another F-4A seemed to swoop up out of the black cloud, and it disappeared overhead as Joe heard yet another boom and saw another cloud of smoke.

He stomped on the accelerator and urged the little metal steed forward, hoping for a shot at some action. The hot sun and high humidity had already caused his jungle fatigues to do the sponge act, but the sweat poured in rivers now as the wiry captain went through the gears. By the time Joe got to the action, the action was gone. He whipped past a couple of tanks and APCs,[2] and next to the road he saw one deuce and a half that apparently had been hit directly by a mortar or rocket. A couple of Huey Cobra gunboats flew in circles over the open area between the highway and VC Mountain.

Joe stopped to check things out when a major, eyes bulging with fear, panic, or both, waved Joe forward desperately.

He screamed, "We're under attack! Get the hell out of here!"

Joe grinned and nodded, taking off toward Kontum. He bypassed the halted column, passing numerous soldiers, rifles, and machine guns out, staring off toward VC Mountain. Joe wondered why they didn't keep moving, but he wasn't there to discuss tactics. The major told him to get the hell out of there, and he decided, if the unit had leadership like that, he might just get plugged by some nervous, scared-to-shit private. He stepped on the gas, zig-

2. Armored personnel carriers.

ging and zagging along the column. Joe saw two columns of smoke still rising ahead of him from bomb strikes.

He laughed to himself about the frightened major and came upon another mortared truck, flames and smoke billowing out of the back end. Joe was flying and didn't have time to brake for the black cloud of smoke obscuring visibility on the road. He passed through the veil and again went sailing into space over the edge of a brand-new five-hundred-pound bomb crater. Joe hit the bottom of the crater and plowed into the soft red dirt with the front end of the jeep.

"Fuck!" he said to himself and sat there in the bottom of the crater, laughing.

Several soldiers ran over to the hole and looked down at the Green Beret.

"Captain," a spec 4 yelled, "you okay?"

Joe laughed, looked up at them, and winked.

The spec 4 said, "We're with an engineer unit outta Pleiku. We'll hook you up and crank you out of there in a minute, sir."

Joe grinned and gave them a wave.

Joe Dietrich made quite a few dangerous rides on that road between the two cities, and even took me on one of them, but the worst ride was one when he was all alone, late at night. Joe was driving from Pleiku to Kontum and had a strange feeling that particular night. His bladder started bothering him shortly after he left Pleiku, and he cursed himself for not relieving himself before leaving. He tried to hold out until he got to Kontum but knew all along that he wouldn't make it. Finally, in the shadow of VC Mountain, Joe pulled over to let nature win out.

He left the jeep running, put it in neutral, and set the undependable hand brake. The night, like before, had been illuminated by a full moon; however, this evening was also plagued by an overcast sky. Joe walked over to some bushes next to the road and looked around. His .41 magnum was tucked into the left side of his belt, as usual when he drove. The Swedish K normally slung around his neck was now in Joe's right hand, finger on the trigger. He felt uneasy, and his eyes strained at every shadow along the side of the road. Captain Dietrich had lived through some tough times and was still breathing. His senses were all on the alert, because something just didn't feel right. He listened. He stared. He even sniffed the evening breeze but couldn't detect anything. Joe maintained his surveillance for a full five minutes and finally slung the rifle around his neck again.

Joe kept looking around while he unbuttoned the fly of his jungle fatigue trousers. He started relieving his bladder, all his senses on full alert. He finished and, feeling a shiver running up and down his spine, he shook as he buttoned his fly again.

The NVA soldier was young, maybe seventeen or eighteen, and his eyes were full of hate and fear as he came up off the ground, the bayonet on the end of his SKS rifle thrusting toward Joe's midsection. One second he wasn't there; the next second, he was trying to thrust a fixed bayonet through the middle of the Green Beret captain. Joe didn't have time to grab the Swedish K or crossdraw the pistol tucked in his waistband. He also didn't have time to think, just react.

Joe had been buttoning his pants using both hands, and his left one came up with a palm block, parrying the bayonet thrust just by his right hip. The NVA soldier had made full commitment with his thrust, and that was his undoing. His right leg had stretched forward full out, and his arms and the rifle thrust deep past the hipbone. Joe's hand closed around the handle of his Ka-Bar sheath knife. It whipped out of the sheath and arched upward, the point going into the NVA soldier's throat just below the Adam's apple. Joe's other hand closed over the barrel of the SKS and held it across his body while the knife buried itself to the hilt. Dietrich twisted the knife as quickly as his hand would move, his heart pounding with fear and adrenaline. The NVA stared into Joe's face, eyes open like two moons, but the eyes had no life behind them. Joe felt something wet and warm flooding his right hand and arm. The body stiffened momentarily and went totally limp. The NVA fell down at Joe's feet, sliding off the end of the knife.

Joe still had to go by instinctive reaction. He was in deep shit, he knew, and he had to get out of there fast. He wiped the blood off the blade on the NVA's uniform and slipped the knife into the sheath, grabbing his Swedish K again. He grabbed the revolver in his left hand and ran the few steps to the jeep, with a gun in each hand. Holstering the pistol, Joe took off with the accelerator to the floor, Swedish K set across his lap. He headed up the road as fast as he could push the military vehicle.

Joe figured that he would just simply have to fly across any bomb craters along Highway 14 that night. When he hit Kontum, Joe started down one street and saw a QC roadblock at the end. Some QCs fired warning shots, and he lifted his Swedish K and let her rip, sending Vietnamese "white mice" diving for cover in all directions. Joe slammed it in reverse and floored it. He whipped the jeep back around the corner and took off, seeking a safer route to B-24. Safely in the compound, Joe finally noticed the dried blood all over his arm, hand, and uniform. He headed for a long, long shower.

When Captain Dietrich arrived at Plei Me, he found that the camp commander was one of those wonderful counterparts who did his best to get rid of any American team commander who came in. That is, he would unless he could find one who didn't mind him getting richer than hell by running the local black market and every scam one could imagine. In fact, good old Dai-uy Ha got eight American SF captains relieved as A team commanders at Plei Me in just one year's time.

When Joe got to the camp, he discovered it was built like one of the old-type SF camps in a triangular shape. Some were also built in star shapes, but unlike Dak Pek, which was so easily defensible, Plei Me offered a good target. A former French army base site, it had been the spot of many battles in the past. Joe had a job to do, and he tried to analyze what was going on and figure out how he could keep Plei Me safe and secure. It had been the site where the Medal of Honor had been won, when overrun by North Vietnamese in the past, and it had been won by an SF captain. Joe would have liked to win the Medal of Honor, but not while his A camp was being overrun.

He noticed that all the CIDG strikers in the camp wore tattered, raggedy uniforms. That was strange, Joe thought; usually every camp had a tailor, and there were uniforms in stock that could be used for replacement. He took a Montagnard interpreter and walked around the compound. Dietrich knew that several sets of Vietnamese eyes were watching his every move, so he just made small talk with the interpreter and pointed at things here and there. Finally, Joe found what he wanted; they passed out of sight on the other side of the Americans' team house, and he found a striker making clay bricks and wearing a very tattered uniform.

Joe said, "Ask him why he has holes in his uniform."

The interpreter spoke to the Yard and then relayed the words to Joe: "Dai-uy, I could have told you. To get any clothes fixed with tailor, strikers have to go to LLDB and buy a ticket."

"Buy a ticket!" Joe raged. "What the fuck do you mean, buy a ticket?"

The interpreter said, "The LLDB make us pay for everything."

"Everything?"

The interpreter smiled. "Dai-uy, many men do not fight as hard on operations, because they are afraid to get wounded."

Joe was astounded, and it showed on his face.

"Why?" he asked.

"Because we have to pay five hundred piastres[3] to the LLDB to ride in medevac helicopter to hospital."

"What?" Joe raged. "I cannot fucking believe this shit!"

That was the only anger the wiry captain allowed himself to show, however. Joe Dietrich didn't handle problems by shouting or kicking doors in, generally. He would coolly and calculatingly figure out the best way to deal with the situation. The first thing he would do would be to contact Lieutenant Colonel Marquis, the B team commander at Kontum, and make him aware of the situation. Joe went to the team's commo bunker and had the radio operator send a coded message on the single-side-band radio. An hour later Joe received a reply, an emphatic order to cooperate fully with his Vietnamese counterpart.

---

3. Five hundred piastres, or dong, were roughly equivalent to U.S. four dollars and twenty cents.

The rest of the day was uneventful, but the following day started early. A loud explosion rocked Joe's bunker, and he scrambled out of bed right at daybreak. Weapon in hand, he was ready to rock and roll, but leaving his bunker, he was met by several team members also scrambling out. They stared at a billowing cloud of dust and smoke and saw flames starting to crackle up.

Joe turned to the sergeant next to him and said, "Don't tell me, that was the camp tailor's place?"

The sergeant lifted a cigarette to his lips, offering another to Joe.

He replied, "Okay, sir, I won't tell you, but that is damned shore what the fuck it is."

Joe walked into the team house, mumbling, "Out-fucking-standing."

Several tired-looking sergeants, pouring cups of coffee, trudged in the door.

One looked at Joe and said, "Captain, I believe your X ray is trying to make a fucking statement."

The man looked past Joe, and Joe turned his head. An LLDB sergeant with a sneer on his face stood in the door of the team house.

He said, "Dai-uy, Dai-uy Ha says you come now to LLDB team house."

Joe laughed and sipped his coffee.

He said, "Sergeant, you go tell your CO that he does not give me orders and try to make me lose face. If he wants to talk to me, he can come here, or ask me politely to come over there."

"No biet!" the little NCO said.

"So you don't understand, huh," Joe said. "Well, I guess your boss is just going to have a long wait."

Angry, the sergeant turned and stormed away.

Another American, pouring coffee, didn't even look up, but said, "Guess Captain Dietrich just made a statement, too."

Little did Joe know that the actions of those two days were the beginning of the famous "War of the Counterparts at Plei Me," as Joe jokingly called it.

Joe received another communication from B-24 to come in for a meeting, so he hitched a ride on a chopper and went in.

The meeting wasn't long, and after its conclusion, Joe, opting for a good time and good company, headed for the NCO Club, much looser and more enjoyable than the uptight Officers' Club. He sat in the dark-plywood-paneled bar sipping a can of Budweiser, speaking to several sergeants from the 4th Infantry Division and a couple of guys in civvies who were from FOB 2 C and C Central in Kontum.

"Yeah," Joe said to the SOG guys, "I heard some of your cohorts ripped off a mechanized one-seventy-five in Da Nang and wouldn't let a colonel into the compound to claim it, 'cause he didn't have a need to know."

One of the two responded, "Yeah, I heard about that."

Joe said, "I just took command of Plei Me, and I want to find us a tank in case we have to E and E."[4]

One of the 4th Division sergeants grinned and, leaning over, quietly said, "Captain, can we go outside and talk privately?"

The two men got up and walked out into the hot, steaming night air. They lit cigarettes and talked in the lee of the club.

4. Escape and evade, in case the camp was overrun.

The sergeant said, "I can't believe you said that, sir. I just happen to have an IG inspection coming up, and we have an M-Forty-eight tank we have to get rid of, fast. I'm the first sergeant of a Fourth Division infantry company, and my old man doesn't need to get his ass reamed. He's the first good company-grade officer we've got in since I've been here."

Joe laughed and said, "Know what you mean. Well, Top, I'll be happy to take that tank off your hands."

The sergeant gave Joe a wink and a slow smile. "Captain, I'll be happy to let you, but we don't have to get rid of it so bad we'll give it away. We could use a nine-millimeter automatic and a thirty-eight."

Joe said, "No sweat. You save that tank for me, and I'll be back in less than a week with your weapons."

"Fuckin'-A, sir," the first sergeant replied, "the tank's yours."

Joe replied, "Good. Write down your name and unit for me. I'll look you up when I get back."

"Where you going?"

"Okinawa," Joe said.

Joe returned to Plei Me the next morning, flying in on a loaded Huey. A Jarai Montagnard woman riding on the same chopper carried two fully packed Army duffel bags. As soon as the chopper landed at the camp, Joe summoned an interpreter and asked the woman what she carried. She opened the duffel bags and showed him that they were packed with carton after carton of Salem cigarettes.

Joe said, "Ask her why she is carrying these."

The interpreter laughed and said, "Dai-uy, I know why. The LLDB make us buy things when we go into town or pick them up."

He spoke quickly to the woman, and she replied.

He continued, "Dai-uy, she buys cigarettes for thirty-five piastres and Dai-uy Ha sells them for one hundred and eighty piastres."

"Fuck," Joe said and headed toward the team house.

He ran into a sergeant driving a jeep with a 106-millimeter recoilless rifle mounted on it. He slid to a stop by Joe.

The sergeant said, "We been moving this all over camp like you said, Captain. The LLVC don't fuckin' like it too much, but tough shit."

Joe laughed. "Well, Sergeant, keep moving it around. Dai-uy Ha wants it cemented in next to the LLDB team house, so I told him we have to move it constantly or the VC will zero in on it. I'm not going to give that little bastard anything he wants. Have you seen him?"

"Yes, sir. He and his sweeties are interrogating a prisoner a patrol just brought in. It's just some poor Yard villager that wandered out too far. They're in the LLVC team house."

"Thanks," Joe said, heading toward the team house.

He entered the team house and was greeted by the sight of a well-muscled, nude Montagnard man seated in a chair, his back to the door. The room was filled with laughing Vietnamese LLDB team members. The prisoner's body quivered as one of the LLDB sergeants turned the crank on a U.S. Army field telephone. One wire running from the phone was apparently wrapped around the man's testes and penis and the other was attached to his head. Little acrid plumes of blue smoke swirled out of his black hair and wafted toward the ceiling. With all that, the Montagnard refused to scream or even whimper.

That, however, didn't prevent Joe Dietrich from screaming. He flew into an immediate rage, grabbed the sergeant turning the crank, and slammed him against the bamboo rattan wall so hard that he flew through the wall backward with a resounding crash. Joe shoved another out of the way and grabbed the field phone, smashing it at the feet of Dai-uy Ha.

He raged at the camp commander while untying the wire from the near-dead prisoner, "We obey the rules of the Geneva Convention, you dumb-fuck, sawed-off son of a bitch! You will treat all prisoners the way I want any of my men who get captured to be treated! Do you understand, motherfucker? Do you understand?"

Dai-uy Ha nodded his head meekly, but his eyes belied the hatred he felt for all Americans, and especially this latest captain who dared stand up to him. I suppose, of all military commanders in this world, he actually figured he would intimidate SF officers into succumbing to his graft and corruption. I suppose the same man would have walked up to Mr. T and tried to give him a quarter to shine his boots.

Joe commanded, "Have this prisoner taken to the dispensary immediately, and he will live. You understand, asshole?"

Ha again nodded affirmatively, but Joe Dietrich had really made him lose face, the ultimate "no-no" for Vietnamese males. The little black-marketeer would not soon forget this day and this humiliation.

The following day, Joe carefully typed out a phony official-looking USAF directive on some stationery he "borrowed" while in Pleiku. He put a phony signature block of a nonexistent Air Force lieutenant colonel and signed it. The directive was posted on the camp bulletin board, and it read that indigenous personnel would no longer be permitted to ride on USAF aircraft flying to and from Special Forces A camps.

Obviously, this phony directive would put an immediate end to Dai-uy Ha's appointed couriers picking up and delivering his black market goods for him. He was furious. Dai-uy Ha stormed over to the American team house and demanded to see Joe Dietrich. Nobody could find him.

"*Choi oi!*" the captain fumed, cussing in Vietnamese. "*Choi doc oi! I want see Dai-uy Dietrich right now!*"

Choi oi translates to "sun-rock," but in Vietnam is about the equivalent of screaming "motherfuck!" in English.

The sergeant first class who was the earpiece for the camp commander's ravings had been in four SF groups and took the man's screams with mild amusement.

Speaking calmly with a slow South Texas drawl, he said, "Now, tie a knot in it, Dai-uy. Ah'm sure old Captain Dietrich didn't desert, so he's boun' ta be aroun' here somewhars. I'll find 'im fer ya'. Wanna beer?"

The angry officer stiffened up and said, "No."

Grinning, the sergeant grabbed a can of Bud and walked out the door.

Joe Dietrich turned to page two of *Stars and Stripes.* The latrine door opened, and he looked up at the Texas-born NCO.

"Howdy, Cap'in, figgered ya' might be in here."

Joe grinned and said, "Yeah, I'm just creating a Dai-uy Ha."

The sergeant laughed and said, "Speakin' of the devil, sir, the sorry fuck's in the team house raisin' holy hell, wantin' you right now."

Joe laughed and said, "Tell him I'm working on a report right now about the condition of the camp's fighting force and bring him here."

The NCO laughed again and replied, "Here? You want me to bring him in the shitter?"

Joe laughed and nodded affirmatively.

"Yes, sir."

A minute later, the door opened and the Vietnamese captain stepped into the latrine, shocked look on his face as he saw Joe, smiling, trousers down around his ankles. Face red with fury, veins bulging, the man stiffened and kind of vibrated all over. He turned but stopped at Joe's words.

Joe heard the sergeant's muffled chuckle outside as he said, "Wait, Dai-uy, don't get mad. It is a custom in my country for men to have business meetings in a bathroom. Women are not allowed to be there with us men: It is not their place."

The VN officer turned around and gave a slight grin, saying, "Oh, I did not know that, Dai-uy. I am very angry about the paper from the Air Force. Did you tell them to do that?"

Joe smiled and said innocently, "Oh, no. They had some indigenous troops in several camps who stole things off aircraft. That's why."

Dai-uy Ha replied, "Oh. Maybe you can talk to Air Force."

Joe said, "I will, Dai-uy, I'm working on it right now."

Joe's face turned red, and he grunted, straining and passing a stool. Suddenly realizing he had been had, Dai-uy Ha also turned red, but with outrage. He turned and stormed out the door, Joe's laughter ringing in his ears.

The next morning, Joe jumped out of bed, again at daybreak, to the sound of another explosion. Again he ran out of his bunker, weapon and gear in hand. Again he and the other startled team members looked at the billowing smoke and dust of yet another building just blown up. The cloud cleared a little and they saw that the latrine was destroyed.

Joe shook his head from side to side, and he and his men filed into the team house. They sat down and laughed at the stupidity of the LLVC, when they heard angry shouts in Vietnamese and objects started striking the sides and roof of the team house. The team members rushed outside, armed to the teeth, to find the LLDB team yelling and throwing clumps of clay at them. The Americans dodged the clay and started laughing. The laughter became infectious, and they laughed even harder. Pretty soon numerous Jarai Yard strikers joined in the laughter, and the VN got even angrier. Not wanting to get hit by a wayward clump of red clay, the Americans ran back inside, holding their sides with laughter.

Less than half a week later, Joe Dietrich returned from Okinawa on an Air Force C-141 Starlifter. In his bag were a Smith & Wesson .38 Special and a Browning high-power 9-millimeter automatic he had gotten from old contacts with the 1st Special Group. He also got some great advice on handling counterparts from his old team sergeant from Okie, M. Sgt. Rich Perkins. Joe had been in the 1st Group in 1966 and 1967 and went to Korea on Task Force Campbell, a joint operation with the South Korean Army that they called Operation Dok Soo Ri. Very simply, they searched for North Korean infiltrators and saboteurs. Rich Perkins knew a lot about counterpart relationships and was very clever in handling indigenous personnel, so Joe, being a damned good officer, sought the counsel of the wise and experienced noncom. Joe laughed like crazy when Sergeant Perkins told him what to do with Dai-uy Ha. He couldn't wait to return to Plei Me to try it out. Joe stopped in Pleiku and made the trade with the 4th Division NCO for the tank. He told the sergeant that one of the NCOs from his team would be sent out to pick it up.

The morning after Joe returned from Okinawa, he awakened with a smile for the first time in months. This day he was going to put Rich Perkins's plan into play.

He also made sure he had his war bag ready in case Perkins's plan didn't help his counterpart relations. Joe's war bag was his E and E contingency in case his position was overrun. He carried a small bag with him that contained amphetamines tied up in a condom, a Montagnard loincloth, and a Yard knife as well. If shot down, overrun, or feeling capture, he would head west, figuring he'd meet less resistance. If captured, Joe figured he would speak only German and claim that he was a German correspondent living in Montagnard villages and writing stories about the people and their culture.

Joe got a quarter-pound block of C-4 plastic explosive from the team engineer/demo man, along with some time fuses and a blasting cap. With these in hand, he wandered out after breakfast and walked along the camp perimeter very slowly. Joe watched out of the corners of his eyes, and was happy to discover that Rich Perkins was indeed correct: He was definitely attracting a crowd.

Joe used his sheath knife as he spent the entire day moving very slowly around the perimeter. He poked the knife in the ground here and there. Occasionally he would seemingly find the spot he was looking for. Joe stopped, dug the knife into the ground, and dug out a small hole. He would then place the C-4 in the hole, attach the blasting cap and a time fuse, and light it. After the plastic explosive went off, Joe returned to the little crater and poked around it. He then would cover it back up with loose dirt and tamp the dirt down. Following that, Joe would return to the team house, curious Vietnamese eyes following his every move, get another block of C-4, and begin all over again. After four days of this and a number of little covered-up holes around the perimeter, Joe finally stopped. He then would sneak up into the camp machine-gun tower with binoculars and laugh while watching the LLDB and their coolies studying each hole, trying to figure out what he was doing. Joe kept watching, and they checked the holes on a regular basis, day in and day out.

The Vietnamese were not the only ones who noticed these strange happenings.

During Saturday dinner, one of the NCOs said, "Hey, Captain, what the hell's the deal with the C-4 and the holes in the perimeter?"

Joe laughed and said, "Little trick I learned from my old team sergeant in Okie. The holes serve no purpose whatsoever, except to keep the LLDB curious as hell. It keeps them out of mischief and our hair. For the first time since I've been here, we haven't had one negative incident this week with the LLDB."

Everyone laughed, and another sergeant said, "That's it? That's fucking it? You mean your blowing little holes in the ground was nothing, and them fucking gooks are shitting themselves and jumping out of their asses, sir, and it ain't nothing?"

Joe grinned.

Another sergeant, still laughing, said, "Captain, you are SF."

Later that day, Joe again had to leave for a meeting in Nha Trang at 5th Group headquarters. He spent the night at the BOQ and prepared to leave the next morning after breakfast. Joe was on his way to the airbase when he bumped into 5th Group chaplain Spry.

The minister said, "Captain Dietrich, how you doing?"

Joe smiled. "Just great, Padre. How about you?"

"Fine, fine. You guys sure give me plenty to keep me busy at my job."

Joe grinned.

The chaplain got a serious look and said, "You know, I just got in from Pleiku. I want to warn you: You've been relieved."

Joe smiled a knowing smile and gave the chaplain a little wave.

He said, "Thanks, Chaplain. I expected it."

When Joe arrived at Pleiku a few hours later, he received word to report to the C Team XO, Major Howe.

Joe reported to the major and Howe replied, "Captain, the decision has been made to make a command change at Plei Me. As of right now, you are the liaison between us and the Fourth Infantry Division."

"Major," Joe said, "what's the real story?"

Howe grinned at him and said, "S-Two got word that the Vietnamese want you dead. I believe, more specifically, your counterpart does. He's an asshole."

Joe laughed and said, "Yeah. What else is new?"

It wasn't long before Joe, wanting to get into more action, got a chance to go north to Kontum and command the B-24 Mike force. He got into action immediately. He went into a hot LZ after a pinned-down 173d Airborne lieutenant in An Lao Valley. Joe and the Mike force launched out of Bong Son and went into the valley, fighting their way in and out. They rescued the thankful young man and returned him to Fire Support Base Corregidor.

To Joe, though, something much more dramatic than risking life and limb happened on that operation. An incident occurred that brought the Special Forces constant situation and challenge to his mind. Several of his Yards had real problems running and charging in battle, as they had worn out their oversized tennis shoe–looking boots. Joe tried everywhere to get them more, but they were unavailable. CIDG were just bottom priority. One of the strikers was exceptionally brave, and Joe, frustrated, took off his own boots and gave them to the man. After Joe and his Yards were extracted to safety, the barefooted American captain bummed another pair of boots from a 173d Airborne company. The greatest thing that happened in that incident was the respect the Mike force strikers gained for their new CO. From then on, Joe could do no wrong.

Captain Dietrich, like others, got enraged quite often with the constant barrage of directives, messages, and requests for reports from B-24 command. One day he got particularly perturbed with the commanding officer, so he decided to make another famous Joe Dietrich kamikaze jeep drive. He figured, in fact, he would kill two birds with one stone. One, he'd drive out some of his anger, and two, he'd ruffle some feathers that needed ruffling as often as possible.

Highway 14 was a major line of communication that started far south of Pleiku and ran northward, paralleling the Vietnamese/Cambodian and Vietnamese/Laotian borders. It ran through Kontum and went through the mountainous highlands, finally turning eastward at Ben Giang and ending near the ocean at Hoi An. The highway through most of the jungled area was hard-packed dirt, and during the height of the war was, for practical purposes, impassable between Kontum and Ben Giang. If the road was not traveled the jungle would quickly overgrow it and choke it out. Additionally, between Kontum and Ben Het the road was constantly ambushed and mined by the VC and the NVA, so nobody but they used it. In fact, most of the area was a "free-fire zone," so anyone spotted in it got fired on.

What a perfect place for Joe Dietrich to barrel a jeep down at breakneck speed. And so he did; and so he did not hit any mines or get ambushed, both of which were miraculous.

Nobody was more shocked than the main gate guard at Ben Het when he saw the bespectacled Green Beret officer suddenly pull up to the camp's main entrance. He let Joe in, and Joe headed directly toward the team house. Joe saw the American team leader walking along with the camp commander, Dai-uy Ha. Ha walked away briskly while Joe got out, shared greetings with the other captain, and explained to the amazed man why and how he got to the camp. They went into the team house and shared a beer.

Joe sipped the beer while watching out the team house door. He finally spotted Dai-uy Ha leave the LLDB team house door, so he quickly bid *adieu* to the USSF team members and walked outside. He waved at the Vietnamese captain and walked over to him, broad smile on his face.

"Hello, Dai-uy, how are you?" Joe said very cheerfully.

Ha greeted him with a forced smile and said, "Hello, Captain Dietrich. You really drive jeep here from Kontum?"

Joe nodded and offered the little man a cigarette. The man accepted, and Dietrich lit both.

"Why you come?" Ha asked.

Joe looked around and said, "Oh, the colonel asked me if I wanted to command another A team, and I said sure. He asked where, and I heard you were the camp commander here now, so I said, I'd like to go to Ben Het if Dai-uy Ha is camp commander there. He told me to drive up here and see how I like it."

Joe gave Ha his biggest toothiest smile, and the LLDB strained a smile on a face that looked like it was masking extreme illness.

Joe clapped him on the back and said, "Yeah, this looks great! Just fine! I think I'd love it here!"

I met him, right after that, at the joint Dak Seang operation. It was almost immediately following that that Joe took over as CO of Dak Pek. His first official duty was to have a contest with our assistant intel sergeant and me. It was an important contest, which tested our combat-readiness skills to the max. The sergeant went first, I went second, and Joe went last.

The little Jeh boy stood there smiling, the sound of the fast-rushing Dak Poko almost drowning out our thoughts. The sergeant lasted about ten seconds and now lay on his back on the sandy riverbank at the fording point. I gulped and took the rope tied to the big water buffalo. I leaped up on his broad back and kicked him in the ribs. He took several steps toward the water and decided to get rid of the second pesky critter astride his back: me. I tried to dig in with my calves and heels but had no "leather" to grab on to. I remember looking at those big, broad, wicked-looking horns as I passed over them. I landed, quite unceremoniously, on my back, half in and half out of the rushing water.

It was finally Joe's turn, and he smiled at the two of us, swung up on the bull's back, and lightly touched his heels to the animal's rib cage. Apparently ready to cross the ford, the big animal calmly walked into the river, Joe Dietrich atop his flanks, grinning at us all the while. The water buffalo did not buck or rear; it just calmly walked through the rushing water. Halfway across the river it made it then and still plodded ahead, with Joe now laughing loudly, water swirling up over the tops of his jungle boots and soaking his trousers to the knees.

Just at that time, almost two thirds of the way across, the water buffalo decided that he wanted to cool off. Joe had just turned to give us a full grin when the big beast suddenly lay down in the churning white water. Joe disappeared under the foam, bobbing up; a second later, his camouflaged cowboy hat was flopping down around his ears. He made his way back to us on the bank while we held our sides laughing, but in all fairness Joe rode the beast much longer and farther than either of us. He passed his first major test at Dak Pek.

I really respected Joe as a team commander, and I liked him as well. I believe he regarded me as immature at the time, and didn't quite understand what I was about. There was no doubt in his mind, or in others', that I was an alcoholic. In fact, years later, Joe Dietrich told me that team members would have arguments over waking me in the morning, as they were afraid of getting shot until I had drunk some Montagnard rice wine or whiskey in the morning. He also informed me that he was concerned that I had a death wish, as I constantly volunteered to take other team members' places on operations and seemed a little "too" gung ho.

Thanksgiving was fast approaching when Joe received still another directive, as did all the other A detachments under B-24's command. The directive from the B Team commander, Lieutenant Colonel Marquis, commanded all members of all A teams to celebrate a traditional Thanksgiving dinner of turkey, cranberry sauce, etc. It further stated that there would be no exceptions: All personnel would celebrate such a holiday meal.

The directive was the stimulus for numerous jokes and comments by guys on the team, as well as on all the other A teams. As mentioned, we went through one period where we had to eat elephantburgers for a while. The idea of us having turkey and other Thanksgiving trimmings was, to say the least, ridiculous at best.

We had cause for further laughter and jokes when team members got to read the response message that Joe Dietrich sent back to the "old man." It was not only hilarious, but it also further endeared the captain to his men, as the NCOs, and officers as well, got pretty sick and frustrated with the orders, commands, directives, and requests from "chairborne rangers" sitting in offices in cities while our asses were constantly on the line.

The message Joe sent to Kontum essentially read:

*To: Commanding Officer
          Operational Detachment B-24
          Company B
          5th Special Forces Group (Airborne), 1st
          Special Forces*
*From: Commanding Officer
          Operational Detachment A-242*

Company B
5th Special Forces Group (Airborne), 1st
Special Forces
Re: Your Msg
Subj: Traditional Thanksgving dinner for all
            personnel
      Operational Detachment A-242 has canvassed all
available local supermarkets, grocery stores, and other
businesses, but turkey and other traditional Thanksgiving meal items mentioned in your directive have not
been available on local shelves for at least two weeks
and are not expected to be resupplied in the near future.
      Request Operational Detachment A-242 be
granted permission to subsist on water buffalo steaks,
rice, and other locally available foodstuffs in lieu of
traditional Thanksgiving dinner.

                                    All is well,
                                    Joseph K. Dietrich,
                                    Captain, Infantry
                                    Commanding

   Ning was in my bunker sewing a cloth sheath to hold
my bamboo knife sheath on the back of the thigh of one of
my tiger suit uniforms. She was bent over picking up a
spool of thread she dropped when I stepped in the door.
Ning looked up at me smiling and screamed. Laughing, I
quickly reached up and yanked the field protective mask
off of my face. What the Army called a field protective
mask, civilians referred to simply as a gas mask, which
makes a lot more sense to me, even if it does protect
against some radioactivity or biological threats, too. I had
not worn my issued mask yet, but I would be using it soon
on an operation, so I wanted to ensure that it fit properly
and was in good order.

Joe had asked me to be his number two man on a major operation, but I was not allowed to reveal where we were going yet, as it was classified. I could only tell the Yards that we would be facing numerous Soviet tanks, concrete-reinforced bunkers, and that the NVA employed gas in the area. I had to give our strikers a crash training course in the use of gas masks and the M-72 LAW, light antitank weapon. Most people know it as a foldout, or actually telescoping, portable bazooka.

Ning took the gas mask from my hands and said, "What is this? Make you look same-same *beaucoup* big bug."

She giggled, and I just looked at those shining, laughing eyes. The only things we had in common were that the Vietnamese hated us both, we were in the thick of the nastiest war known to man, and we lived to make love or laugh with each other. I was actually entranced by her smile and those dark eyes. I realized that I really was in love with her.

I pulled her to me, and we stared deep into each other's eyes. Our faces came slowly together and our lips met, softly at first, then passionately. She pushed her body up against mine, and I did the same, trying to melt right into her body.

With Ning, it was always much more incredibly intense than ever before. I believe that there was a need to try to be inside a "womb of safety," of tenderness, of love —all the things that I tried so hard to block from my life at that time.

I was in the throes of alcoholism that began at the age of fifteen. Chemically, my whole emotional being was totally out of whack. With alcoholism, when you are still actively drinking, because of the chemical imbalance and aberrant behavior, you suffer from extremely strong feelings of guilt and loneliness, too. I was suffering from those feelings, like many other alcoholic or addicted veterans who poured it in like sponges in Nam, and I spent a lot of my time trying to anesthetize that incredible emptiness with more booze and occasional drugs.

Besides the fear of death I was denying and constantly challenging, I was having an affair with someone, although I had married right before going to war. I was totally frustrated by higher headquarters; fellow Americans putting us down for doing what we believed in; the political machine that ran the war instead of military leaders doing it; the press, who seemed like they were our enemies; the South Vietnamese, who were always trying to kill me; the North Vietnamese, who had a bounty on my head, too; but most important of all was the unbelievable frustration I had over the plight of the Montagnards and the discrimination that was levied on them by the Vietnamese. It seemed like I hated everybody except Ning and the rest of her people. What I didn't know then was that I really hated myself.

I awakened with a start and started laughing. Something tickled my ankle and calf. It was a wet tongue. I looked down at the foot of my bed and saw the outline of a moving body under my blankets. I heard Ning giggle and felt her tongue on the inside of my calf again. I jumped, and she laughed heartily. I grabbed something quickly, just before she, still giggling, moved back up. She looked at me, again wearing the gas mask, and gave out a little squeal and much laughter. She pulled the mask off and grabbed me in a bear hug.

"You be big bug again!" she said while giggling. "No be big bug. Scare me *beaucoup!* Just be Don, man I love number one thou."

We kissed again, and I knew I was going to get a late start on training my strikers.

There was still plenty of sun over the emerald valley when I lined a platoon of strikers up in the little training area I had built next to the camp runway. Nhual was with me, and we had already instructed them in the use and quick employment of the gas mask.

I told him to line up, facing a series of cardboard silhouette targets I had stuck into soft dirt at the base of a small hill by the runway. I made sure I was upwind from them and suddenly pulled out two CS gas grenades, pulled the pins, and tossed them onto the ground in their midst.

There is no word in Jeh for "gas" or "mask," so Nhual yelled, *"Dei ei johom!"*

It literally means, "No breathe!"

The youngest warrior there, a twelve-year-old with several kills to his name already, pulled his mask out and calmly yelled a repeat of Nhual's words. The rest of the men looked confused and scared, but when they got a faceful of gas, they showed sheer panic. Red-rimmed, teary eyes opening wide, they started to run in complete fear, but I fired my CAR-15 into the dirt in front of each man who ran. I have to hand it to the young striker, as he got his mask on fine, cleared it, and ran to others, trying to help them and show them how to get their own masks on. They were too panicked, however, and even firing in front of them could not stop them from trying to escape the choking, burning gas. The strikers streaked for the river one hundred yards away. All were rubbing their burning eyes vigorously, and three of them started vomiting from breathing the potent gas in deep breaths. Nhual and I sat down, laughing to ourselves, then started off for the river.

We reassembled the platoon and marched them back

to the training site. The Yards, normally very proud and brave, hung their heads in shame—all of them, I should say, except for the twelve-year-old man, who would be a boy in America.

When we got to the training spot, I called the platoon to attention and called the young warrior out. No words were needed. We had hired several prostitutes in Kontum to make us black triangular neckerchiefs with the words "Dak Pek Strike Force" on the back. All the Americans wore these scarves around their necks. The only others who got to wear them were Montagnard strikers who were rewarded with a scarf for an act of extreme bravery. Although what the young warrior did was not exactly death-defying, I removed the scarf from my own neck and tied it around his. He smiled broadly, his shoulders going back, his chest puffing out. The others seemed to slump over in shame. This was a twelve-year-old being rewarded for do-ing what they were supposed to do, but they acted too cowardly to do it. The scarf worked as an excellent motiva-tional tool for the mercenaries, who normally received only pay but no awards or formal recognition.

I walked over to one of the silhouette targets while Nhual instructed the men to be seated and take a five-minute cigarette break. I pulled out two more gas gre-nades, popped them, and tossed them in the midst of the strikers. Every single man yanked out his mask and pre-pared to put it on.

Simultaneously, numerous cries of *"Dei ei johom!"* rang out from the men. One man had problems with tight-ening the six straps on his mask but was helped by another striker next to him, who had already gotten his on and in place. In seconds they stood there in place, proudly looking at each other and at me, clouds of burning gas swirling about them.

I gave the men the thumbs-up sign and told Nhual to assemble them on line. They quickly lined up, and I had him tell them to open fire on the silhouettes. Wearing a protective mask was one thing; shooting at and hitting an enemy while wearing one was another. They fired and missed, reloaded and fired; some missed, some hit; they reloaded and fired and hit. We practiced over and over.

I worked two platoons that afternoon and dismissed the last at suppertime.

I went to the team house and grabbed some meat from the freezer and two cans of beer from the bar. I went to my bunker, but Ning wasn't there. I found her at her aunt and uncle's. They had raised her, as her parents were killed by the Viet Minh.

I had earlier paid a dowry to Ning's uncle for her betrothal, and it was probably the biggest dowry ever paid in the tribe. There were pigs, chickens, beads, cloth, rice, and other niceties, and it made the old couple rich. I was their hero.

According to Jeh custom, a betrothed couple lived together for one year but were not allowed to consummate their relationship during that time. They were allowed heavy petting, but that was it. Ning and I cheated as often as possible.

I took her by the hand, and we headed up to the American hill, directly above us. Her aunt and uncle lived in a bunker where the security platoon's perimeter was located on the extreme western end of the American hill's perimeter. We crossed the hill and headed down the driveway, down beyond the parade ground and camp headquarters, the barber shop, the school classroom I had created, and the storage building. Behind that was the camp dispensary and helipad. We passed out the main gate, nodding at the sentry in the sandbagged guardpost.

When we got to the Dak Poko River, I handed Ning the food I brought in the little rucksack, along with my CAR-15 rifle and the rolled-up Army poncho liner I had with me. I picked her up and waded across the fording spot of the fast-rushing river. I set her down on the other side, and we kissed.

"Why you do that?" she asked.

"Because I love you and always want to kiss you," I replied.

"No, no," she said. "Why carry me across river?"

I chuckled. "We call that being a gentleman, honey. I was keeping you from getting wet."

She gave me a perplexed look and said, "No understand. I get wet all time. I get dry soon. No sweat. Water feels good and washes feet—me, my feet."

I grinned and said, "I know. I know."

She said, "We come back, I carry you across river. Keep boots dry and uniforms dry, same-same."

I started laughing my head off as Ning and I headed into the tall grass. The sun was getting close to the peaks, and the rays slanted across the valley, slicing through the low-hanging clouds here and there. We walked along the trail and stopped suddenly as a green bamboo viper suddenly appeared in the muddy trail in front of us. It was the deadly snake that Americans called a "step and a half"; its neurohemotoxic poison was so deadly that, if bitten, you were only supposed to be able to take a step and a half before dying. Soldiers jokingly told others that you should light up a cigarette, if bitten, and try to finish it. Earlier, I had run into several more on an operation and was almost struck in the hand by a banded krait, which I killed, and was almost bitten by a spitting cobra as well. I had some close calls with several poisonous snakes there, as I have a number of times since then. Ning was with me, however, so I didn't want to take any chances. I wore my .357 magnum in the quick-draw holster, so I drew and fired. The snake's head disappeared.

A few minutes later, Ning and I were at the base of the hill upon which her family village was located, Dak Tung. We walked up the path and entered the gate five minutes later. We were greeted happily by the villagers. My six FULRO-assigned bodyguards, as always, shadowed us while we walked and entered the gate behind us. They were also greeted happily by the villagers, but the people kept their distance from the sentries; however, several young women handed them vessels of water.

The village chief walked up, smiling broadly, and we shook hands in Jeh custom, shaking with the right hands while grasping one's own right wrist with the left hand.

Knowing he spoke no English, I smiled happily while saying, "Nice to see you again, you crusty old Viet Cong motherfucker."

Ning knew what I said and laughed heartily, as she knew I spoke the truth. This old fart played both ends against the middle, trying to be friends with us and the local VC and NVA. A real wimpy politician, he must have studied under the LLDB.

With Ning translating, I told him we wanted to borrow a cooking fire and bunker that night and spend the night in the village. He offered his own bunker, but I turned it down. We were soon given a fire and bunker, and Ning prepared the food we brought. I went into the bunker and placed the four candles I brought in the four corners. I then spread the poncho liner out on the packed-mud floor and pulled out the two cans of beer, pouring them into the two canteen cups I also brought. I removed the little flower I had carefully carried in the one canteen cup and removed the .50-caliber shell, turned it upside down, and placed the flower stem in it. I poured a little water in from my canteen.

Ning brought our food into the bunker and smiled when she saw what I had prepared. She slipped off her *atok*, and I slipped out of my clothes as well. We didn't speak at all. We just stared at each other and ate the meal slowly, seated cross-legged in the candlelit little bunker. Ning knew that I was going on my most dangerous operation, and I knew that there was a damn good chance that Joe and I might not be coming back alive. We kept staring and eating and simultaneously dropped our food and melted into each other's arms. I laid her back on the poncho liner and started kissing her skin very slowly and softly. In two days I would leave, but this night would be slow and patient. Unless Charlie elected to make it so, it would not be a night of war. It would be a night of love, slow, patient, tender love—the exact opposite of combat.

I was very gung ho in those days, but still understood and appreciated the absolute stupidity of war. It was either a caricature of a strong entity physically standing up to a bully, two entities who got too frustrated or were too weak to communicate effectively, or simply two entities who had little value for the individual makeup of their countries, which was human lives. To me, the love was a much-preferred act to the war. Now I cannot get enough of the love and hope I will never hear of war again.

Plei Trap Valley was one of the strongest NVA positions in all of South Vietnam. It was the major infiltration point of the Ho Chi Minh Trail going into South Vietnam right below the triborder region where the borders of Laos, Cambodia, and South Vietnam came together. Prior to the Tet Offensive in February 1968, the NVA built a road through Plei Trap Valley and infiltrated Soviet-made tanks and trucks through it to use against the cities of Kontum and Pleiku. It was due west of one of Dak Pek's sister camps, Polei Kleng. We had been putting Arc Lights, B-52 carpet-bombing strikes, on it daily, but the NVA simply plowed around the five-hundred-pound bomb craters and the road was just a little more crooked than before. They also had log- or concrete-reinforced bunkers every twenty meters along the road, so NVA soldiers or bundle-carriers could hide in case of an air strike anywhere along the expedient jungle road. In addition, they built wooden bridges that passed about six inches to one foot underwater at numerous stream crossings. Most of the mountain jungle streams were crystal clear, but it often rained, causing them to become muddy. At that time, aircraft would fly overhead without detecting bridges for vehicles at each stream crossing. The three main streams were the Nam Sathay, the Ya Tri, and the Dak Hodrai, and they went the length of the valley, which ran to the southwest, with one branch coming in from the northwest and the other from the northeast.

The most important thing about Plei Trap Valley was not the superhighway for infiltrating troops, tanks, and equipment. It was not the numerous bunker complexes. It was not that it was so well defended that any American soldiers who tried to infiltrate the valley had gas thrown on them. It was not the big ammunition caches. Recent intelligence reports indicated that there was an expedient bamboo-constructed POW compound in the valley, in which

American POWs were held and interrogated, awaiting transfer to bigger prisons in Laos or North Vietnam.

With one hundred ass-kicking Jeh strikers, Joe Dietrich and I were to go into that never-before-conquered enemy stronghold, fight the tanks, fight the gas, fight the NVA soldiers, fight the fear, and locate and rescue the American POWs. We were to combat-assault in on the first helicopters to the western end of the valley, right on the Laotian border. Behind us, other CIDG companies from several A camps, including Polei Kleng, Duc Co, Plateu Gi, and Plei Djerang, a Mike force company, and elements of the 4th Infantry Division would execute a sweep-and-clear operation, three units abreast through the big valley. We would act as a blocking force to stop NVA units from making it back across the border, retreating hopefully in front of the Allied sweeping units. Additionally, we would be providing flank security to keep other NVA units from coming into Vietnam from Cambodia and attacking our moving units. We would move into the valley in a massive helicopter assault, following a big artillery preparation, which would follow on the heels of a B-52 strike as well as pinpoint air strikes. We would have jet air cover standing by to support us at airbases at Tuy Hoa and Cam Ranh Bay. Locally, we would also have helicopter air support by teams of Huey gunships and Cobra armed helicopters. On top of that, several Spookies[5] would be available. Hopefully we would have some 105- and 155-millimeter howitzers emplaced after we were in the valley awhile. From the get-go there would be 175-millimeter howitzer artillery

5. Spooky (of Puff the Magic Dragon) was a converted C-47 prop plane armed with four computer-controlled electronic Gatling guns capable of firing eight thousand 7.62-millimeter bullets on a selected target in a minute.

support from the combined base camp set up next to the Polei Kleng A camp.

First, our units would be helitransported to Polei Kleng, where we'd set up base camp right outside the camp's perimeter. We would bivouac in the midst of the other units mentioned, and launch out of there after receiving our operations order. Only Americans were aware of the operation and were to be the only ones to know where we were going until it came time for our briefing.

Joe and I couldn't wait. Keeping the LLDB from knowing where we were going and what we were doing might finally be the break we needed to accomplish something really great. Maybe the Plei Trap Valley would become our "Valley of Victory." Eternally optimistic, Joe and I thought and dreamed of it that way. As idealistic as we were, we both still had that little underlying fear that if it went the way of most operations in Vietnam, it would not become the "Valley of Victory"; it would become the "Valley of Tears."

I hopped onto the back of my black-and-white Overo paint horse. The war bridle on him was made of braided rawhide, and his tail was tied in an overhand knot, the sign of war. He had five red coup stripes on each foreleg and had red handprints on his neck and rump. Two eagle feathers were braided into his white mane. I wore red war paint on my face, the paint shaped by placing my fingertips in the paint, then smearing it outward from the center of my nose. It resembled the talons of an eagle. Additionally, my eyes wore a raccoon mask of black paint. I wore a breechcloth, porcupine quill–decorated soft-soled moccasins, a bone hair pipe breastplate, sheath knife, and a lone eagle feather in my long, long black hair.

I looked to the far hilltop and saw a whole regiment of

U.S. cavalry being led by an officer in fancy buckskins and with long blond hair. He rode a magnificent chestnut with four white stockings and large blaze face.

A yell turned my head, and I saw my woman run out of my bullhide lodge. She was gorgeous, the morning sun radiating off her copper skin and shiny black hair. She smiled with tears in her eyes and ran to my pony, jumping up into my arms. I held her, and our lips met, her long hair cascading over my bare shoulders.

I opened my eyes and looked at Ning, her eyes closed as she kissed me good morning. I pushed her back and shook with the morning chill. I laughed as I thought of romantic movies I had seen and two lovers awakening and making love first thing.

I chuckled and Ning said, "Why you laugh?"

I grinned and said, "Hollywood. I have to go pee, honey, and brush my teeth."

She smiled. "Me do same-same already. I put brush you and tootpaste outside door. Water, too."

I smiled, and bending halfway over, went out the door of the bunker. I looked at the brilliance of the rising sun and the steam rising out of the valley. Anywhere but there, I would call it morning fog, but it was steam.

An hour later, Nhual and I hauled a number of empty fifty-five-gallon drums from the motor pool. We had loaded them on a three-quarter-ton truck and tossed them off at the training area. The Yards were already assembled, smoking and telling simple jokes, producing numerous cackles of laughter in various pockets in the crowd. As Nhual directed, they set up the drums in line where we normally had the silhouette targets.

I then spent the day teaching, or reteaching, all the strikers who were going on the operation on how to shoot the M-72 LAW light antitank weapon. I am quite sure by then that they were all convinced we were headed for Hanoi, after the extensive training on the use of gas masks and starting to review the employment of the M-72 LAW.

The LAW was a small, lightweight tube device with a rocket inside. The olive drab tube had caps on both ends. To fire, pins were pulled and the caps removed, one of which swung down on a piece of string. The other folded down and became a shoulder rest. There were actually two tubes, one inside the other. After the caps were released, the smaller tube was pulled out until it caught and latched in place. On the top, a plastic pop-up sight flipped up with a spring-loaded device. The distances were marked in red and illustrated meters to the target. A rubber-covered, squeeze-type trigger was ahead of the sight.

The rocket inside the little disposable bazooka would, when fired, leave a tremendous backblast, which in itself was dangerous. The danger was similar to that of the original bazooka and the more modern 90- or 120-millimeter recoilless rifles.

Unlike the bazooka of World War II and Korea, which contained a shape charge–type explosive shell, the M-72 LAW had an incendiary rocket. When fired, the rocket would hit its target and explode, generating instant and intense heat, which would literally melt the armor of a tank, for example, while it penetrated through a hole it created. The hole would be only a few inches wide, but through it shards of red-hot molten steel, from the tank's side and the rocket itself, would ricochet around the inside of the tank. Invariably, ammunition supplies or fuel supplies in the tank would be ignited, causing a secondary explosion. Additionally, the pieces of hot metal would go through the bodies of those men inside the tank, bunker, or vehicle. The concussion from the exploding rocket was also deadly.

After firing the M-72 LAW, the user would simply discard the hollow tube.

We fired numerous LAWs that afternoon; then we issued two M-72 LAWs to each striker to carry on the operation. We spent the rest of the day issuing rations and ammunition as well.

The next morning I awakened before dawn and, yawning, stumbled to the shower. I let Ning sleep, as I awakened because of nerves and anticipation several times during the night, and heard her quietly and softly sobbing, her tears falling silently onto her pillow. She didn't want me to know how much she worried about the upcoming operation. I couldn't let her know where we were going, but Ning could tell this was possibly going to be the "mother of all battles." I was probably somewhat apprehensive in my manner, and we certainly were preparing for this operation as we never had before.

I showered and shaved, knowing it would be the last time for weeks. I looked at myself in the mirror. That day my eyes were green. Some days they were light brown. My face was very tanned and very thin. Mustache and eyebrows were very dark brown, with my short hair best described as brown, period. I was six feet, two inches tall and weighed one hundred and fifty-five at that time. All the climbing mountains and training before Vietnam had made my muscles like thin steel cables. I closed my eyes and prayed for safety and victory; then I threw in some words for the Yards and my family back home. Opening my eyes, I looked at myself and glanced quickly about, feeling I was being a bit narcissistic.

I smiled at my mirror image and said to the guy there,

"If they finally get you this time, Bendell, you've got to go out SF, no matter how fucking scared you are."

I suddenly felt moved to pray again. I do not believe there were atheists in the American fighting forces in the Vietnam War, except maybe when some guys went away on R and R.

I again closed my eyes and dropped to one knee, with my usual flare for the dramatic.

I said, "Dear Lord, I know I will be walking through the valley of the shadow of death, and I know, God, there's a good chance those little motherfuckers will get me this time. Pardon my language, sir. If I have to go out on this one, please let me rescue any POWs who are in there first, and don't let me go under acting like a pussy, God. In Jesus' name I thank you and pray. Amen."

I don't pray like that now, but I do pray a lot. Some won't understand language like that in conversation with one's Higher Power, but anyone who was SF will understand perfectly. It was almost like being in an alien world. We developed alien habits and an alien pattern of thinking. Thank God, though, the universal, ever-present spirituality of the warrior was still there. It always was there when it came time to face the enemy. It was time to count coups. It was time to enter the valley of the shadow of death. It was time to enter the Plei Trap Valley.

When I set the bouquet of flowers on the pillow next to Ning, along with my wallet and Special Forces ring, her eyes opened slowly, and she suddenly sat up, wide awake. I had just made it to the door. Tears started dripping down her cheeks, and she forced a brave smile.

"My warrior goes to battle," she said softly.

"And your lover will come home to hold you and kiss you all night long," I replied with a smile.

She smiled.

"You do that with me," she said, holding up the flowers, "you give me love *beaucoup*, but you leave bunker. You go jungle, and you tiger, not my Don. You killer."

I thought about her words and looked out the bunker door. I wore my tiger suit, ammo harness, and pack. My CAR-15 was in my left hand. I lit a Lucky Strike, took a deep drag, and looked back at my love.

"Honey, that's why I came here," I said.

She got up and walked over to me, suddenly bursting into tears and rushing into my arms. I kissed her and smiled down. Even in tears, her eyes were filled with laughter, gaiety, and mirth. Ning started to speak, but I gave her a shushing gesture and touched my index finger to her lips.

I kissed her eyelids softly and said, "I love you ten thou."

She grinned and said, "Love you same-same. Good-b——"

I touched her lips again, interrupting her words, and said, "Do not say good-bye, honey. I will be back in two weeks. We make love *beaucoup*."

She grabbed her *atok* and started to put it on, but I gently grabbed her hand and shook my head no.

"Stay here, please. You'll hear us fly away."

She gave me a big wink, something I had taught her. I smiled, winked back, turned quickly, and headed up the steps.

I wasn't being melodramatic then. I had a lot of men to help Joe Dietrich with. We had to get them loaded and out of there, quickly and efficiently. I had to concentrate on my job, and I didn't want Ning watching, stealing my thoughts away from work. She was too distracting to me, way too distracting.

An hour later, our ten Huey helicopters flew, in formation, between Dak To and Ben Het. The crew chief and door gunner on each bird carefully scanned the jungle below, looking for any signs of enemy fire. It was kind of a thrilling feeling seeing Hueys, rotors spinning, just a few meters away from us, in front and behind. Below them and my feet, which hung out the door, the bomb-pocked jungle flashed by quickly thousands of feet down. As we finally descended toward the big LZ next to Polei Kleng, I heard strikers in my chopper murmuring about Plei Trap Valley. As far away as we were from Dak Pek, my men had heard of the major stronghold and knew that's where we were going.

This was incredibly amazing in light of the fact that these simple, primitive people would sometimes ask an American questions like, "How many days does it take to walk to your village?"

That was the only way they could relate and try to understand how far away we lived.

While Joe headed toward the Polei Kleng A camp, I took over and had the men set up a perimeter first, digging in foxholes and supplementary positions. They then put up their tents, dug latrines, and, of course, started cooking food. We didn't have to send out any patrols, ambushes, or listening posts that night, so I felt good knowing all the men would be well rested. The 4th Infantry Division had taken responsibility for area security at the base camp staging area.

I poured a steaming cupful of hot water into a plastic bag full of dehydrated chili con carne, my favorite LRRP ration. I ate the delicious meal and swallowed it with a canteen cupful of hot tea as a chaser. Gunfire started, and I turned my head to see the Montagnards throwing empty

C ration cans up in the air and shooting at them. Joe and I brought our pistols and quick-draw holsters with us to wear while in base camp, so I lit up a cigarette and walked over to join the Yards. Nhual tossed a can up, and I whipped out my Smith & Wesson in a quick draw and fired from the hip. I missed by a mile.

Behind me was the A camp of Polei Kleng, and across the broad valley, to the east, were some jungle-covered mountains. Right next to the operation's base camp was a mechanized infantry unit from the 4th Infantry Division. Nhual and several other Yards took turns shooting cans while I reloaded my revolver. Finishing my Lucky, I flipped the hot ash off the end and ground it into the dirt. I crumbled the remaining tobacco up between my fingers and let it blow away with the breeze. I then rolled up the paper into a tiny little ball and flipped it off into the weeds. Field-stripping my cigarette like that was a habit I picked up in basic training and was a good one that stayed with me. There was no use hanging signs out to signal the enemy where you were and that you were somebody who smoked American-made cigarettes. Nhual tossed a can up for a couple of strikers, and I flipped the gun out again and fired twice, missing the can clean again.

Seeing a chance to try to make me lose face, a young LLDB sergeant from Dak Pek walked up, with several Vietnamese backing him up. It was rumored that this brat's crooked, wealthy father had bought him his stripes and that he had been the biggest troublemaker on the LLDB team since arriving at Dak Pek. He was also wearing an Army Colt .45 automatic on his right hip.

I sensed something was in the wind, so I quickly ejected my spent shells and reloaded my revolver, spinning it backward into my quick-draw holster. Trying to appear relaxed, I actually had every sense tensed and ready for trouble. It always happened when this LLDB NCO jerk came around Americans. My tension was completely sparked by the cocky, smartass grin on the face of the young Vietnamese.

The American cowboy was the biggest hero of the Vietnamese soldiers. Vietnamese punks tried to imitate cowboys and practiced quick draw for hours. The brat NCO was one of those punks.

Obviously showing off for his grinning buddies and trying to make me lose face, the sergeant stopped in a gunfighter's crouch twenty feet in front of me.

He said, "Trung-uy, you-me have showdown, same-same cowboy."

There it was. In a split second I realized several things: One, the sergeant was positive that I wouldn't take him seriously and would back down, thus losing face; two, the LLDB had a bulky, heavy .45 automatic to draw, while I had a .357 magnum revolver in a quick-draw holster; three, I had grown up with heroes like the Lone Ranger, Roy Rogers, and the Range Rider and had practiced quick draw, like many American boys, since kindergarten.

Without hesitating—I couldn't afford to—I stared at the Vietnamese, pulled out a cigarillo, and lit it slowly, executing my best imitation, to date, of Clint Eatswood's "man with no name."

I grinned, teeth clenched around the little Swisher Sweet, and said, "Okay, Trung-si. Nhual will count to five in Vietnamese. When he says 'Nam,' we draw and fire, and you die. Count, Nhual."

Nhual said, *"Mot! Hai!"*

In a panic, the young sergeant threw his hands up in the air, pleading, "No, wait! Stop! I joke you!"

Squinting over the cigarillo, I calmly said, "Keep counting, Nhual."

"Ba! Bon!" Nhual went on.

I really wasn't scared. Just like being in combat with bullets screaming by my head, I went into a calm, a dead calm. I was in a vacuum bubble, shielded from fear, worry, or concern. After this incident ended, if I lived, I would become shaky and very frightened, but right then I felt as calm as could be.

In a panic, the LLDB NCO clawed for his gun before Nhual got to five, and I dived straight forward, drawing at the same time. My revolver came out smoothly, as it had thousands of times before. My right thumb eared back the hammer, and at the same time my left hand grabbed my right hand, providing extra support under the gun's grip. I looked along the sights and instinctively thought "Fire at center mass," the words I had heard so many times in training. I tightened my stomach and diaphragm as my body and elbows hit the ground. Looking across the sights, I saw that my bullet was going to hit him dead center in the chest; then I noticed that he still had not gotten his .45 automatic out of the holster.

The realization suddenly hit the profusely sweating NCO as he let go of his gun as if it were a red-hot fire-brand and stared wide-eyed down the mouth of my gun barrel. Sweat poured off his face, and his Adam's apple bobbed up and down. His color turned from yellow to pale white. I couldn't help myself. I just lay there grinning as I heard the sounds of numerous chuckles arising from the ranks of Montagnards while I held the sights on the little man's breastbone. I finally stood up, still pointing the gun at the punk's midsection, and I walked slowly forward. He could hardly swallow, I could tell, as I got closer, until the barrel of my gun was a scant six inches from his navel. He seemed to be trying to form words but couldn't. He also looked like he was going to cry.

"Trung-si," I said, cigar clenched tightly between my teeth, "you ever try to make me lose face again, I'll kill you."

I brought the .357 magnum up in a vicious swing and smashed the LLDB sergeant across the bridge of his nose, cartilage giving way with a crunch. The man flew backward, piling into his three buddies, and the four of them fell on the ground in a big heap as all the Jeh warriors roared with laughter. I turned and noticed that my six bodyguards, the silent shadows, all lowered their rifles, and I grinned, realizing that the rich brat was going to go down, even if he had beaten me. I was also grateful that those six fearless men assigned to protect me hadn't intervened, knowing that I needed to do what I did to put the LLDB in his place.

The LLDB was picked up by his cohorts, and looking like he was having trouble walking, and with his nose streaming blood, he wobbled away with the embarrassed trio.

I walked over to my canteen and took a drink, not letting anyone know how much trouble I was having keeping my own sea legs. I took another long drink and swallowed two salt pills, knowing I had lost a lot of salt and water from my system from the usual perspiration and the additional sweat as well. I watched as the Jeh, still laughing, started tossing cans up and firing at them once more. I started experiencing horrendous diarrhea cramps, followed by waves of nausea, and my legs shook uncontrollably. I figured nobody could see them, and I just gutted it out until the feelings passed. I really did feel like I had suddenly developed a horrible case of the flu, but I knew it was my nervous system reminding me that once again I had acted like an asshole.

Nhual walked over to me and whispered, "You stay here, by yourself, until the feelings of fear go away, huh, Don?"

Nhual was one of my best friends and called me by my first name when nobody else was around. He never even considered acting familiar around others, though.

I grinned at him and said, "Ba Nua, you are definitely a warrior."

He smiled and said, "We men act brave, but no smart man does not get scared when he faces the enemy."

I nodded and shared a swallow of water with him from my canteen.

Quietly I said, "Well, my brother, I am ready to go out and pretend like everything has just been a lot of fun and games."

Nhual and I rejoined the strikers and started firing at cans again. Sunset was approaching, and a few who hadn't eaten already started fixing meals.

I heard a vehicle roar behind me and I turned, seeing a 4th Division second lieutenant riding in a jeep from the mechanized infantry unit that was bivouacked next to us. I walked over and grabbed another swallow of water while they approached, and I dropped my big bladder canteen on my jungle hammock. The red-faced officer jumped out of the jeep in a rage, and I couldn't help but notice his spec 4 driver trying hard to suppress a grin. This struck me funny, so I grinned myself.

The "leg" officer screamed, "Cease fire! Cease fire!"

The Yards ignored him and kept shooting, so I said quietly and calmly, "Cease fire."

Nhual quickly translated my words, and within seconds all the Dega stopped firing and looked to me for instructions. As usual, I was proud of our strikers.

As mentioned, when we went into the field, we wore camouflaged tiger suits with no insignia, rank, or badges of any sort. Joe and I wore camouflaged cowboy hats. Joe Howard wore a black felt Stetson shipped from his native Texas, and most of the guys wore floppy hats. We didn't wear our berets, steel pots, or flak jackets, but we did wear our black scarves.

"Can I help you, Lieutenant?" I asked innocently. "You from that mech infantry unit?"

"Yes, I am!" he screamed in a total rage. "Who's in charge here?"

"I am," I replied calmly, really amused at this wet-behind-the-ears guy who had veins popping out on his neck and forehead.

No wonder people make jokes about lieutenants, I thought, glad that I was due for promotion to captain in half a year.

"Soldier, you and your men are shooting up my LRRP patrol on that mountain!" he yelled, pointing. "What the hell do you think you're doing?"

I started laughing and said, "We're killing time, and there's no fucking way we're shooting your LRRPs. That mountain is two fucking miles away and covered with triple-canopy jungle."

"Who authorized you to fire a weapon, soldier?" the young officer screamed even louder.

I laughed again and dryly replied, "Congress, you dickhead; we're at war, in case you hadn't noticed."

Still yelling, the lieutenant raged on, "I had to call in a grid clearance yesterday to shoot a rabid dog!"

Even more red-faced and really about ready to explode or come apart at the seams, he continued, "You can't just shoot when you want to!"

I really laughed at that remark and said, "No wonder we're losing this cluster-fuck they call a war."

"Who are you, smart aleck?" he demanded. "Who's your commanding officer?"

"I am, Lieutenant," Joe Dietrich said with authority, walking up to us from the side toward Polei Kleng.

The lieutenant snapped his head around to spot Joe walking up.

Joe said, "Captain Joseph K. Dietrich, Operational Detachment A-Two-forty-two, Company B, Fifth Special Forces Group."

Knowing Joe was quite capable of handling this situation and totally amused anyway, I just watched and grinned broadly. The embarrassed second balloon snapped to attention and saluted.

"Don't salute me in a combat zone, you asshole!" Joe snapped. "You might just as well hang a bull's-eye on me!"

"Yes, sir," the lieutenant replied, "but this soldier was very—"

Joe interrupted, "Lieutenant, this soldier is a first lieutenant who is due for promotion to captain very shortly and who could eat you for breakfast."

The second louey started to speak but couldn't find words, then mumbled something, jumped in the jeep, and drove off. I bet his driver was doing all he could to keep from wetting his own pants with laughter. Joe and I stood there watching after him, laughing our butts off.

We both walked over to the cooking fire by my place and accepted two steaming cups of hot chocolate from Nhual.

"So, what's the good word, sir?" I asked.

"Another delay," Joe replied disgustedly. "No air support. The Twelfth Tactical Fighter Wing in Cam Ranh Bay and the Thirty-first Tactical Fighter Wing out of Tuy Hoa are both nailed down by typhoons."

I was furious, to say the least. The LLDB commanders in the operation had been briefed that day, so I knew that we would have to get into Plei Trap at first light, or the NVA would already have received word from their Vietnamese spies and infiltrators what was going down. The American POWs would be moved or, worse yet, instantly killed.

I replied angrily, "And the Viet commanders need time to warn the NVA before we go into Plei Trap Valley! I can't believe I put in for an extension!"

"Oh, come on, admit it, Don," Joe said, teasing, "you're having a lot of fun, aren't you?"

I passed gas.

As most SF troopers did during times of extreme frustration during the Vietnam War, I tried to joke around about it, but this time it was a little too much.

I had a lot of friends who had been captured. We all did in SF. We also took care of our own, and there was and still is a certain feeling of helplessness in regard to POWs. Getting captured was a common thing for Special Forces and was a constant fear of each man. The North Vietnamese had an automatic bounty for the live capture of Special Forces soldiers during the Vietnam War. They wanted our deaths to be slow if they chose to kill us, and they wanted to torture as much intel out of us as they could, as they knew SF NCOs and officers carried a lot more valuable intel and were a lot better informed than the run-of-the-mill grunt in a conventional unit. We also made better bargaining chips in peace talks and their grand extortion plans for war's end, as we were legendary soldiers of the war, canonized in film, print, and books.

I remembered Joe telling me he was in Kontum in a meeting with Lieutenant Colonel Marquis, the B team CO, when the intel came in about the POWs being held in Plei Trap Valley.

The idea for the operation came up, and Joe told me Marquis walked back and forth, wringing his hands in excitement, saying, "I just can't wait to see the headlines in *The New York Times:* 'B-24, 5th Special Forces Group Rescues American POWs'!"

We didn't really get concerned about newspaper headlines ourselves, though. We had the opportunity to save some comrades, especially some of the brave brass-balled Air Force pilots who had saved our lives so damned many times. Now the LLVC would surely pass the word on to the wrong party, some of them on purpose, and our operation would be compromised.

I had wanted Plei Trap Valley to become our "Valley of Victory." I worried that it would turn into the "Valley of Tears," but now I was concerned that it would become the "Valley of Death." The NVA had been in there a long time and had plenty of opportunity to fortify their positions. They had gas, helicopters, Soviet MiG jets, antiaircraft weaponry, rockets, mortars, artillery, small arms, fortifications, booby traps, and lots of cover; and more important than anything, plenty of warning to prepare for us. Our good friends and allies the LLDB would surely see to that.

I was so mad, I could kill. I don't know why, but it was a common thing in Special Forces. Someone in SF would take a company of Montagnards, Chinese Nungs, Laotian Mnongs, or whomever, all armed with World War II–vintage weapons and other equipment. They would then wipe out a heavily armed NVA force, capture a regimental commander and headquarters, underground hospital complex, and numerous weapons and personnel. Because they were working opcon under the 101st Airborne, Marines, 173d Airborne, 25th, 1st, 4th, or whatever infantry division, or some other conventional unit, they would soon have articles in the newspapers back in the world that their unit accomplished that deed.

Sometimes an SFer would spend six months building up trust and friendship with local Vietnamese peasants, and then a conventional unit would come in with a lax commander and his troops would ask the village chief's respectable daughter to "make boom-boom" for five bucks, and all those months of winning people over would go right down the drain.

Another common occurrence would be like Joe Dietrich's situation at Plei Me. The camp commander had a big, profitable black market operation going and constantly complained about Americans who tried to interfere, and wimpy commanders at B team and C team headquarters wouldn't have the balls to go to the wall for their men and relieved them on the word of the crooked counterparts.

At B-24 and C team headquarters at Pleiku, there were guys with desk jobs getting CIBs[6] thirty days after arriving, when those of us on A teams would get ours up to nine months after being on-site. Many guys on A teams and at Mike forces also had recommendations for medals blocked by deskborne B and C team executives.

As one highly decorated infantry colonel once said

6. Combat Infantryman's Badge, for thirty continuous days in combat under fire.

upon receiving a Silver Star for extreme heroism, "I got this for doing what Special Forces guys do on an average day at an A team."

It was a thankless and frustrating job, kind of like being the best stuntmen in the world, with some real jerk movie stars getting all the credit, then not even acknowledging your help. The one saving grace for all seemed to be a childlike naïveté and positive attitude that it would get better, which it never did. After Plei Trap, there would be another mindless, stupid blunder, but every once in a while we managed to make something turn out right, and that kept us all going.

Additionally, among SF combat people there was a real sense of professional pride in what we were doing and a wink and a nod we could give each other, even if it was another SFer we didn't know. It was a kind of attitude we had that showed each other we were all in it together, and we knew we could do it better than anyone else. The Air Force could give blue berets to their commandos. The 82d Airborne could give red berets to some of their troopers. The Army rangers could give black berets to their men. The U.S. Navy could go all the way with copycatting and professional jealousy and give green berets to their SEALs. All the generals and admirals could do those things, but we knew who really was the very best and who did the real behind-the-scenes, important missions.

Joe started his supper and grinned at me, knowing what was going through my mind, as it had already gone through his own.

He said quietly, almost imperceptibly, "They know we'll be sitting here on our asses tomorrow. You want to go out on a dangerous mission with four Yards and one other

American? You'll probably get your balls blown off or get captured."

I jumped up, excited, adrenaline pumping already.

"Does a bear shit in the woods?" I almost yelled. "Does Howdy Doody have splinters in his dick?"

Joe grinned. "I kind of figured you'd have that reaction, so I already volunteered you."

I was excited, and my voice showed it. "Thank you, sir! What's the operation?"

Joe said, "There's a mountain West of Polei Kleng, and it usually is covered with Victor.[7] A CH-54 Sky Crane accidentally dropped a Fourth Division one-five-five howitzer, and they're afraid it might have fallen into enemy hands. They want a small RT to go into the area and locate it. Nobody can spot it, and recon aircraft have taken a lot of ground fire. A Fourth Division artillery FO[8] lieutenant volunteered right away to go on the mission, and I volunteered you and whatever four Yards you pick who are willing."

Joe and I laughed at that comment, knowing that our motivated strikers would all volunteer to go. I spoke fluent Jeh by then and Joe didn't speak it, so I would leave Nhual with him and knew that the Yards would insist that four of my bodyguards would go, so that took care of that.

The next morning, right after daybreak, I found myself in front of an operations map inside the Polei Kleng TOC. I met the Cloverleaf Division FO who would accompany me, and we determined I had date of rank, so I would command the team. I was going to, anyway: I was SF. The

7. Slang term for VC; just like Charlie, it came from the term Victor Charlie.
8. Forward observer; goes with combat units and adjusts artillery fire.

team op sergeant and intel sergeant briefed us, and I kept noticing little clusters of blue dots in different spots, with no map symbol indicating what it was.

"Sergeant," I asked the intel man, "what are all those clusters of blue dots?"

He said, "Lieutenant, that's a herd of twenty-four wild elephants that hang out in the area. That's where they have been spotted, so if you run into them, give them a wide berth. They haven't trampled anybody or anything, but who knows what the fuck wild elephants will do?"

"Tarzan," I replied with a grin.

He laughed, as did the others in the room.

The intel man said, "Yeah, and Tarzan would know. He's SF, you know."

Somebody else said, "So are Batman and Robin."

Another NCO said, "I didn't know they ate pussy."

The other one said, "Sure, man. Haven't you ever seen Catwoman?"

We all laughed.

Fifteen minutes later, with the fog just starting to lift in the jungled mountain valleys, we lifted off in a UH-1D Huey helicopter. Choppers had been going to and fro all around the camp, but we didn't want to draw too much attention with an insertion. On top of that, there were we two American lieutenants, both with CAR-15's, and four Yards with three M-2 carbines and a BAR. The place was crawling with NVA and local VC, so we were prime targets for capture or annihilation. The decision had been made for the Huey to fly east from the camp, circle back west, and low-level out and up a steep draw near the river that flowed by the camp. The Huey would slow quickly and hover over an area that was full of muck and water and elephant grass, and we would jump out from ten feet. The chopper would take off and would only be visible for those few seconds from those two ridgelines overlooking the draw, so that was the only risk we had of our insertion being compromised, except for the LLVC, of course. The fastest forms of communication in those days were television, telefax, telephone, and tell a Vietnamese counterpart. The chopper would, after dropping us, take off over one of the ridgelines and head way out west of camp, climbing out of range of small-arms fire. It would circle back and land at camp. Any enemy watching from a distance would assume it simply climbed up and over one of the mountain ridges without making a stop.

There were a few problems with that plan, however, that nobody could have known in advance but that became quite obvious to us. We made our insertion, but the Huey pilot was nervous about all the aircraft that had been shot down and shot at in the area. He swept over our insertion point, and we jumped out, with him not hovering but moving slowly forward. We didn't drop five to ten feet, as planned, but each man dropped twenty to thirty feet from the sky, and we sank up to our waists in thick black muck. On top of that, we didn't land in elephant grass. I don't know what it was, but it may as well have been steel bars two or three inches apart. It's a wonder none of us was impaled.

We couldn't move, first of all, and each man struggled for a long time to extricate himself from the gluelike goo. Second, the weeds we were in were about two to three inches in diameter and as strong as bamboo. They were two or three inches apart and about ten to fifteen feet tall. The stuff was immovable, and all I could picture was that herd of elephants plowing through that natural prison and squashing each of us like a grape.

We communicated and located each other by whispers and tried to get the stuff to move, but no one was successful. The stuff was too thick and too tough to cut with a machete or Yard knife; besides, the stalks were so close together you couldn't swing a machete or Yard knife anyway.

Finally, after listening to my instruction, the Yard next to me unloaded and cleared his carbine. He stuck the barrel through the giant reeds to me, and I grabbed it. With me pulling on the barrel and him struggling to move between the powerful stalks, he finally made it to me. We finally were able to grab the sling of a second Yard and got him to my location. I then had the first one climb up on my shoulders, holding the powerful stalks. The second one, using us as a ladder, climbed up on the first one's shoulders and spotted the closest dry ground. He pointed it out, and I took a compass bearing on the direction. We then leaned against the stalks, and they swayed forward. We finally got the team to dry ground using this method, but it took us several hours and pounds of sweat just to make it fifty meters to dry ground.

We took a canteen and cigarette break there, our backs together in a circle, each man facing outward. We were on the foot of a ridge going up the enemy-controlled mountain. After ten minutes we wearily rose and started up the mountain toward the area where they felt the artillery piece had been dropped. As usual in that hell on earth, the heat and humidity were unbearable, the jungle ingrowing every direction at once, except straight up, and the mountain was so steep and unforgiving that if it had had one more degree of slope, we would've been hanging from the tree trunks, our feet over open space.

The going was slow, the fear ratio high, and the land

torturous. We took a ten-minute break every fifty minutes, always sitting in a tight circle, backs together, weapons pointing outward like the horns of threatened musk-oxen. I wouldn't allow smoking after the first break. We hit NVA bunkers near the crest of the mountain, and they had been in use. There were fresh tracks and signs of the enemy everywhere.

I whispered to the FO, "Our shit's flapping in the breeze, man. If we get hit and have to get the fuck out of Dodge, head due east and you'll hit a stream. Cross it and head north. In fact, go up the edge of the stream in the water; it will be quicker, no wait-a-minute vines or tanglefoot. You'll see the A camp and Allied units in short order."

His eyes were open like saucers, but the lieutenant had balls. I let him know it, too.

I grinned and whispered, "You crazy fuck. You volunteered to come on this mission. Why don't you have jumpwings and a beret, man?"

He said softly, "I am afraid of heights. I didn't want to go up in planes."

I chuckled and said, "Shit, why not? You don't have to land in the fucking things. You jump out when they get up too high and get back on the ground before all the people who stay on the plane."

He laughed quietly and shook his head.

"You SF guys are all crazy fuckers, aren't you?" he said.

I nodded my head affirmatively and said, "Yeah. Guess we are."

I paused, then got very serious and stared into his eyes, saying, "But we're damned good, too. Anything happens, stick with me. We'll get out of this."

He grinned and nodded in agreement, replying, "I believe you."

I stuck a Swisher Sweet in my mouth without lighting it. I guess it was the closest thing to a pacifier around.

I whispered again, "Come on. I'll take point. We need to check the other side of this ridge."

He nodded, and the Yards followed. We heard voices coming right at us, and we dropped. The jungle floor was covered with leaves, vines, grasses, and every other nasty green thing in the world, except maybe crocodiles and counterfeit money. Right then it all became a friend, hiding us well from our approaching enemies. It was a large NVA unit, maybe a company, and they passed over, around, and between us as we held our breaths.

We waited ten minutes after they passed, and I rose up out of the undergrowth, looking all around, as if you could see very far in the jungle. Well, I guess you could if you were Johnny Weismuller or Buster Crabbe.

I stood up and signaled the others. We were in deep shit, and I knew it. We must have made it into a regimental staging area, and I figured we must have been surrounded by hundreds of North Vietnamese regulars who luckily didn't know we were in their midst. I started questioning the sanity of my extending for another tour and requesting a transfer to MAC-V SOG. At that point, I knew, if I passed gas, it would come out as a high-pitched whistle. We checked the other side of the ridge, then headed back toward Polei Kleng. We ran into another company-size perimeter. I stuck my hand into the ashes of a cooking fire and pulled it out right away. It was hot, and parts had been doused with water. It told me two things: First, the obvious; second, we were on a mountain with streams below. If it was doused with water, the NVA probably carried canteens. In addition, I could assume they were well equipped.

More voices, so I pointed at the opposite side of the ridge from Polei Kleng, thinking that side would seem less dangerous and threatening to the enemy. We dived again into the morass of greenery. It was an NVA patrol, and we all held our breaths once more, until they passed out of hearing.

We headed back toward the camp and made it to the river with daylight still left. We had to cross an open area, but there were too many NVA about to make me feel comfortable with that open-river crossing. The stream was muddy and running bank-full from recent storms, so I led the little patrol into the rushing water, and we moved across, swimming underwater or wading with our heads sometimes barely out and sometimes under.

We finally made it back, not having seen hide nor hair of the artillery piece. We went straightaway to the TOC at Polei Kleng and were debriefed, then returned to our bivouac sites.

I reported to Joe and turned in for the evening, wondering how many times they would put off our assault into Plei Trap Valley. It would be several more days, but we finally got to go.

The valley was prepped, and Joe went in on the very first chopper, the first American to set foot in the valley without getting zapped or captured. He had me go in on the last chopper. The situation was dangerous, very dangerous, so Joe had an RTO and a Prick-25 radio with him and another RTO and radio with me. The LLDB asshole with us had his own PRC-25.

Nhual went in with Joe, so he could translate for him, and the ballsy captain started setting up a security perimeter around the LZ immediately but had Nhual direct three Yards to accompany him, and they walked down from the hilltop landing zone onto the partially hidden jungle road. The small patrol moved up the road so Joe could check things out. Two of his men tripped booby traps, while my chopper landed, and a third man, on the perimeter, got impaled on a punji stake along the edge of the LZ. We had just come in on a combat assault and had to call a dust-off in right away for three wounded men. Besides the one who got nailed by the punji, another stepped on a "toe-popper,"[9] and the third got nailed in the crotch and waist by a Bouncing Betty.[10] Helping the Yard medics give first aid to the strikers, I thought about our wonderful LLDB friends and their big mouths.

We immediately set up a solid perimeter, and Joe sent patrols out in every direction. The dust-off came in to pick up our wounded. This was all done after Joe Dietrich came back from his personal patrol down "the highway," as we called the enemy's road cut through the jungle. Joe found a couple of small ammunition caches and reinforced bunkers along the road, every twenty paces.

We spent several days setting up company perimeters and sending out patrols in our AO, but our first night was an experience I'll never forget. I went to sleep shortly after dark. At about midnight, however, the noise of an engine brought my eyes open like a blind flying up. I slipped into

9. The NVA or VC placed usually a 7.62-millimeter bullet upside down on a nail sticking up through a board. The bullet, fixed in a groove, stuck straight upward and was buried under a skim of dirt in a trail. If a person stepped on it, the foot pressure would push it down and make the primer hit the bullet, like a firing pin. The bullet would explode up and penetrate the man's foot.
10. An antipersonnel mine that sent an explosive ball about waist high, where it would explode.

my jungle boots and slid my gear on, my eyes straining into the blackness of the jungle. I heard more engines, and they were headed toward me. I shivered and had to stand up quickly and relieve my bladder. I sensed strikers doing the same as I, but I knew they would look to me for leadership. The eeriness of those engine noises in the middle of thick jungle, right on the Cambodian border, was one of the most spine-chilling experiences you could ever imagine.

Joe's voice startled me. "Soviet tanks coming this way, Don."

"No shit?" I said, awe and wonder in my voice.

"Soviet T-Seventy-two battle tanks, I think," Joe replied.

"How in the fuck do you know those things, Dai-uy?" I asked.

Joe smiled in the darkness. "Remember, I ran from tanks, shooting at me, when I was seven. It's a sound you remember. You educate yourself about things."

I said, "You ran from what?"

Joe replied, "Tanks."

I laughed and said, "You're welcome, Captain."

He started chuckling and said, "Fuck you, Bendell."

Trying to joke back but getting too serious, I said, "It sounds like Ho Chi Minh might do that to me tonight."

Joe said, "We can't see, anyway. Let's just lie here and listen."

And so it was, our first night in Plei Trap, which might better have been named Death Trap. We lay among the greenery, blanketed by a blackness, penetrated only by swarms of mosquitoes. We listened as Soviet tanks revved their engines and pulled into secret jungle hiding places along "Gook Highway." We heard them start and stop and wondered if those steel tracks would end up crushing us in our poncho liners, lest we close our eyes and drift off to sleep, but that's exactly what we did. We didn't get crushed beneath the tracks, but we did eventually drift off to sleep, a fitful sleep, a sleep filled with steel monsters and things that go boom in the night.

The next morning, Joe returned to his spot on the other side of the perimeter from me. Being a good commander and tactician, he kept our time together to a minimum, to ensure that both of us couldn't get taken out by one mortar round, hand grenade, or burst from a hidden sniper. I felt terrific pain right in the center of the small of my back. I grunted and rolled over. I had been stabbed before in a fight and still bore the scar on my left thigh, and it felt just like that. Nhual ran to my side as I rolled onto my stomach, and he jerked my pants down with little ceremony. Several Yards gathered around and jabbered incessantly.

Nhual yanked my razor-sharp Jeh knife out, sticking the point in the cooking fire, and said, "Trung-uy, a bug digs a hole into your back. I must cut it out with knife."

"Are you shitting me, Ba Nua?" I snapped.

He grinned and said, "I wouldn't shit you: You are my favorite turd."

"You've been listening to SF NCOs too much."

I thought of every B movie I ever saw, or at least every Western B movie, I should say. I pictured the hero getting shot by an Indian arrow, then having his buddy cut out the arrowhead with a hot knife while he bit down on a piece of leather. I couldn't find any leather, so I gritted my teeth, as Nhual pulled the big blade with the red-hot tip from the fire and aimed it at my tailbone.

In my big battle at Dak Seang, I saw one of my bodyguards get his eye shot out by an AK-47 bullet and take four claymore pellets in his shinbones. He not only kept fighting and carried wounded Yards to the medevac helicopter, but he even grinned at me when I gave him one of my cigars and lit it for him. Drunk one day at Dak Pek, I accidentally amputated the end of a seven-year-old Jeh boy's finger while giving him a ride in a jeep. He never even cried.

I knew that I could not make a peep, no matter how much it hurt, or the Yards would lose respect for me. I lit a cigarette and started smoking it while Nhual cut the burrowing bug out of my back. The pain was excruciating, but numerous strikers looked at me, so I smoked and smiled at several as if nothing were happening. Inside my brain, however, I cried and screamed like a little baby. Still playing macho, I stood up and hitched my pants back up when Nhual finished, forcing myself to ignore the pain of the hole in my back.

"Nhual," Joe Dietrich said in a commanding voice as he walked up, "tell everyone to stand still and not to move! Come with me then."

Joe nodded at me and I jumped up, following him, Nhual walking at my side, giving me questioning looks. I looked out across the valley and saw giant B-52 bomb craters everywhere. Joe took me right to the west edge of the center of our company perimeter, near his hammock, and pointed at the ground. I gulped, but Nhual still didn't know what was going on.

Joe said calmly, "We have to get all the men out of here, with all our equipment, quickly and quietly."

"Yes, sir," I said solemnly. "You think it's a five-hundred-pounder or a thousand-pounder?"

Joe laughed, replying, "Don't know, but either one

could blow the shit out of us. I don't know what kind of vibration could do it, so be damned careful."

I shook my head nervously and scampered off with Nhual at my side.

I said, "A five-hundred- or one-thousand-bomb made that little hole in the ground, but it never exploded."

Nhual's eyes opened like saucers as I continued, "Tell all the men to pack up and not run, jump, or throw things. You need to go with Captain Dietrich and tell the company to follow him single file off this hilltop."

Nhual didn't speak but quickly disappeared into the ranks of strikers. Soon all the men were filing off the hill-top, carrying their equipment with them. As I passed near the hole, I spotted Joe kneeling over, so I walked over to him. Sweat dripped off his forehead, but he looked up at me and winked.

He said, "Surprise for Charlie."

He had wrapped tape around a hand grenade and a pointed stick and stuck the stick into the ground next to the hole. Joe had pulled the pin on the grenade and broke one of the two prongs off, so the pin would come out much more easily. He then replaced the cotter device and stuck the stick into the ground by the hole. When I walked up, Joe had attached a trip wire to the pin and I held it in place, while he ran it across the trail and attached it to a tree, high enough to catch an NVA across the thighs or hips but too high for a barking deer or other small animal to trip. If someone hit the wire, the grenade would fall in the hole and detonate on the tail of the bomb.

We started west on Gook Highway, looking for a new company perimeter. Joe knew that the patrols we had out without radios would easily find our trail and follow. We finally found a new perimeter and set up.

The next day I took a ten-man patrol out on Gook Highway and headed west. The other units were sweeping up the valley toward us. There was a stream crossing about a quarter mile from our perimeter, and that's where we had been sending water details for the past couple of days. When we reached the stream, I studied the cleverly built bridge made of poles lashed together and going several inches under the stream's surface. I took pictures of them with a little Minolta spy camera I owned. I also took photographs of deep-rutted Soviet tank tracks in the mud and soil. Stopping at the fast-running waterway, I sent a two-man patrol upstream for security and another downstream.

The upstream patrol came back within minutes, summoning me. Both men were wide-eyed, so something was obviously in the wind. We went around the bend of the stream and there, in the water, was the decaying body of a North Vietnamese soldier, both legs tied to a waterside bush. Beyond him was the decaying body of a dead deer, also tied by the legs to a bush on the streambank. The tactic was obvious. We took our water out of the stream just around the bend, so they had tied the two decaying corpses just above our watering point, figuring the current would pass across the carcasses and maybe infect us with some germs or bacteria. I cut the bloated bodies loose from the bush, and they floated downstream. I called my finding in to Joe.

We continued down the road, and I was amazed seeing that in many places the NVA had climbed giant trees and bent the tops inward, tying them together over the roadway in giant arches. This was an obvious attempt to obscure vision from American aircraft above. I stupidly had the ten Yards on the patrol leave their gas masks at the company perimeter, as well as leaving my own. I started worrying about this as I moved closer and closer toward the Cambodian border.

Just this side of the border, my point ran into NVA in the trail ahead. The NVA scampered into roadside bunkers. Since I had only ten men on a recon patrol, I called in an air strike on the enemy location. The NVA withdrew from the bunkers and headed back toward Cambodia. Afterward we moved forward, rounding the bend into a strip that had previously been defoliated with Agent Orange. The jets had caught the NVA in the open area and stopped a two-thousand-kilo Soviet tank. Using fire and maneuver, we moved across the open area, letting the retreating NVA have it on the western tree line. The truck had been abandoned by them, its tires blown out by shrapnel. I called in an after-action report to Joe and told him I was continuing west. Joe gave me the go-ahead.

We were almost on the border by then, and in a few minutes two Huey Cobra gunships appeared overhead and called me. Joe had called for them to watch over me and my little patrol. One of them called me and warned me that I was almost over the "dotted line." I let him know that was my intention.

He called me back on the Prick-25, saying, "We can't cross that dotted line. Over."

I responded, "This is Bravo. You shouldn't fly support for Sierra Foxtrot (SF) if you can't take a joke. Over."

He called back, acknowledging my statement, and I could tell he was laughing. We kept on into Cambodia, and I kept taking pictures. Many of the bunkers and bivouac spots I came to had been deserted just minutes before, and I was quite nervous. We carefully moved westward, though, and came upon a hidden regiment-size headquarters complex. There were woven bamboo buildings, camouflaged from the air, even bamboo platforms with little square holes in the center. These were latrines, where soldiers squatted down like all the VN did. There were even woven rattan platforms with sleeping pads that apparently served as barracks for platoon-size units. I took pictures of everything and called it all in to Joe, who was on his own patrol to the east of our perimeter.

He had captured a bunker complex and some ammunition from Czechoslovakia and Poland.

Joe said, "Charlie's monitoring everything we're saying, so you better head back. He knows right where you are. Over."

I had been whispering, but I didn't want to chance it anymore. I knew that we were probably standing right in the middle of the killing zone of a giant ambush. People had been in that location minutes before. There were just ten Yards with carbines and a machine gun and me. I figured, no, I knew the NVA were watching me, and either they thought we were the point of a larger unit and they didn't want to pop their ambush until the whole unit got in the killing zone, or they were afraid of the Cobras I had on station overhead.

Screwing with a Huey Cobra was a little like trying to French-kiss a Bengal tiger: Although it might prove to be a unique experience, the aftereffects could be quite deadly.

We headed back toward Vietnam and relative safety; ha, ha, ha. I just wanted to run like hell and let the strikers who could keep up with me run alongside, but I knew that wasn't wise, to say the least. When we finally crossed the border again, I breathed a sigh of relief. I don't know why. There wasn't a little dotted line along the ground, but there was a psychological one. Even though the brass-balled Cobra jockeys above had followed me, I was on an unauthorized excursion into a supposedly neutral country. If my ten men and I got into deep *ca-ca*, officially no one was required to do anything, although I knew the Cobras would have. Also, Joe Dietrich somehow would have made someone go in with fire support. If not, he would have led the whole operation in there to bail me out, and chewed me out later. Joe was that kind of commander.

We moved along the road slowly, carefully watching for ambushes set up to nail us on the return trip. The Cobras got called farther south to support the sweeping company from Plei Djerang who had run into a couple of NVA who shot at them and ran. Companies from Polei Kleng and Plateau Gi were sweeping alongside them, looking for the POW camp as well, and trying to push the NVA into us. Another company from Duc Co, with 4th Division engineers attached, had assaulted into our LZ, after us. Their mission was to destroy major sections of the road, which they were doing due south of our AO.

I passed a jungle-choked hillside to our left, and I felt very uncomfortable. We were on an open stretch of the road, with no trees overhead, but the hillside was steep and thick with trees and greenery, making us very vulnerable to attack from above.

My fears came true almost immediately. I heard a pop and a hissing sound, followed immediately by another. Gas! There were some noises right next to me on the hillside, and I yanked two high-explosive grenades off my webbing and pulled the pins.

I yelled, "Gas! Don't breathe!"

The whole patrol took off down the road at a fast walk, and the first wave of gas hit them before Nhual could translate my words. My grenades went off, and several of the Yards opened fire on the hillside, spraying it with bullets. Everyone, by then, got a lungful of CS gas, and they panicked, taking off at a dead run.

I flipped my selector switch on "auto" and aimed my CAR-15 at the dirt in front of my fleeing patrol. I opened fire, and those men stopped on their tiptoes, as if they had run into a brick wall.

"*Dei chiu!*" I yelled. "Nhual, tell them not to panic! Don't run! We'll get ambushed!"

"*Mi dei chiu!*" Nhual screamed. "*Yuan cong-san chop bal hay!*"

I continued, with my eyes burning and watering like crazy, "It's the CS gas, Nhual! It won't kill us!"

"*Hang ku wia!*" Nhual yelled. "*Dei chiu*, you fucking cowboys!"

Proudly, eyes burning and watering while they were fighting panic, those men held their rifles at the ready and moved down the road at a fast walk. Choking, I followed behind them and called for artillery. Soon, distant 4th Division 175-millimeter howitzers just about leveled the whole hillside.

We stopped at the first stream crossing and washed our eyes and burning skin. After the training accident with gas I had experienced at Camp A. P. Hill in Virginia, and several bouts of pneumonia and pleurisy, I figured my lungs were going to be about as effective as a bikini stand in Antarctica.

An hour later, we took another break at the Soviet truck we had captured earlier. I was surprised that the air strike had blown out all the tires, but the green canvas cover on the back was in relatively good shape. I had been talking to Joe while I worked on removing the metal manufacturer's plate off the truck.

Joe's voice crackled, "Lackey Bravo, did you get the manufacturer's plate off it yet? Over."

"Lackey Alpha, this is Bravo, that's a big rodge. Over," I replied, looking at the black-and-silver four-inch by four-inch stamped metal plate. "All the writing is in French, but it says that it was manufactured in Moscow in 1962. It's a two-thousand-kilo truck, it says. Over."

"Good job, Bravo," Joe replied. "The boss in P-city wants you to stay there and secure the truck. He's sending a Chinook in to hook it out. Over."

I answered, "Alpha, Bravo. We're in a hornet's nest and will damned sure get stung if we sit around here smoking and joking. What the hell's he want it for? Over."

"Probably put it up in front of his Hôtel-Québec. You don't argue with stars. Set up a perimeter and be careful. Over," Joe commanded.

At that time, I probably would have argued with President Johnson, but Joe gave me a direct order, and he was my CO, and he was SF. Arguing with Joe was out of the question, so I did what most good SFers did when frustrated: I grinned.

"PeeWee Lackey Alpha, this is Bravo, wilco. Over," I said. "Alpha, by the way, if you hear some explosions, I have an understream bridge to blow up and a couple of bunkers, too. Over."

Laughing, Joe knew what was happening and he replied, "Roger, Bravo. Understand."

He then told me about the patrol he had been on and the ammo he captured and bunkers. I took some blocks of C-4 plastic explosive out of my pack and some time fuses and a blasting cap. I got a couple of M-72 LAWs from some of the strikers and opened the first LAW, resting it on my shoulder. I made sure no Yards were behind me.

"Ba Nua," I said, "the commanding general of the Fourth Division wants us to stand around guarding this Communist piece of shit so he can put it on the front lawn of his headquarters in Pleiku."

I lit a cigarette and said, "You suppose there could be some NVA hiding in it?"

Grinning, Nhual replied, "Could be."

I fired the first LAW, and the door exploded into pieces. I started laughing as I prepped the second LAW and fired again.

"Get back!" I yelled as I pulled the pins on two HE hand grenades.

I continued, "There may be a gook hiding in the cab."

I ran up to the truck, tossed the grenades in the window, and ran like hell. I dived on the ground, arms over my head, while the cab exploded with both little hand bombs. After that, I attached a block of C-4 to the frame and blew it again. When the big Chinook helicopter came in to hook it out, the truck looked a bit worse for wear. Joe Dietrich fell over laughing as the tangled wreckage passed over him. SF always had to put up with a lot of Sierra Bravo but always seemed to figure out ways to even things out.

An hour or two later we were back at our company perimeter, and this time a Huey helicopter flew in just to pick up the film I had shot along Gook Highway. S-2 had been told what I shot and wanted them. They were to send the unexposed rolls to higher headquarters. The next morning, S-2 called Joe and told him that the pictures I had taken were being sent to Paris.

The following morning I was awakened by gunfire and thought we were under attack. When I found Joe Dietrich, he was calmly drinking a cup of coffee and standing behind a tree. Every few seconds he would emerge from the tree, draw his .41 magnum, and fire several rounds at the wooded hillside opposite ours.

Yards were hiding all over the perimeter. I finally found out that a sniper had opened fire on our perimeter from the other hill. Joe started shooting back at him with his pistol, as the sniper wasn't a very good shot. Joe would fire three times, then the sniper would do the same. Joe would fire twice, so would the sniper. What the sniper didn't know was that Joe called for 175-millimeter howitzer fire on the hillside, which had already been plotted in on the big guns. Joe heard from the artillery that rounds were on the way. He stepped out from behind the tree, fired twice, and waited. The sniper fired twice, and the hillside exploded under a hail of artillery rounds.

The following day we headed toward the LZ to be extracted. Joe moved there first, while I stayed behind with a small patrol as a rear echelon, protecting our ass, which was very vulnerable, exposed to Cambodia. Our patrol spotted some NVA in bunkers along the road. Joe called for an air strike, but the area where the bunkers were was between Joe, with the main unit, and us. Two Yards found a cache that contained a wooden spool of U.S. Army det cord, highly explosive white line that looks like plastic clothesline. We shoved a stick through the spool and they ran along the road and rolled it down the sloping entrance into one of the reinforced bunkers. I ran behind them, tossed two hand grenades into the bunker entrance, and ran like my tail was on fire.

I had already sent the rest of the patrol running full speed past the bunkers to a twenty-five-foot-wide and fifteen-foot-deep bomb crater. I figured the NVA were watching Joe, who was in sight all the time, on the cleared-off hilltop LZ and hadn't seen us. The rest of our patrol ran in front and set up cover fire for us. The two volunteers ran next with the spool of det cord. I followed, going full speed as I ran by the bunker door. One surprised NVA stuck his head out the door as I ran by.

I yelled, "Fire in the hole!"

The Yards, not understanding my words, still knew what was going to happen, and they ducked. I got ready to dive over the lip of the crater, just as the det cord went off and the concussion slammed into my back and sent me flying in a somersault out over the lip and down, down, down onto my back at the bottom of the crater.

Joe, watching all the while, said, "Bird dog, Lackey Alpha, your target is marked. That's my people in that bomb crater. Over."

"Rog-O Lackey Alpha, tell yer folks to keep their heads down. Got two birds comin' down with some big eggs. Over."

Joe said, "They don't have a radio with them, but I think they know to duck. Over."

I moaned, lying on my back in the bottom of the crater, but I smiled as I heard the jets streak in and drop their ordnance.

An hour later, thirteen UH-1D choppers landed and picked us up for the trip back home. I looked down at Plei Trap Valley and thought back to Joe's scouting mission before we came into the valley. He had flown over our area of operations along the border and counted nine visible automatic-weapons positions, drawing fire from most. One position Joe kept flying over, a single rifleman kept shooting at the plane continuously. The gutsy L-19 pilot circled back and flew right above the rifleman's position, barely higher than treetop level. Joe Dietrich opened the door on his side and dropped a handful of bullets directly over the sniper. Laughing, Joe and the pilot left the valley, bullets chasing after them through the sky.

Joe and I didn't laugh, though, as we left Plei Trap Valley. We knew that below us were numerous NVA Soviet-made tanks hidden under trees and foliage. We knew there were dozens and dozens of slanted, almond-colored eyes staring up at our helicopters—knowing eyes with smiles at the corners, realizing they had just done well against their enemy, an enemy who always had to fight with their hands bound behind their backs. Joe and I knew that we had friends below, comrades from our Army and Air Force and Navy, who were bleeding and sick, starved and sore, frightened and depressed, all enslaved in bamboo and barbed-wire cages. We knew that those men stared skyward at our helicopters heading out of the valley, and they wondered if our country would remember them. We knew they saw their hopes flying away with the beats of our rotors.

I thought about shaving off the two weeks' growth of beard and showering away the two weeks of crud. I thought of lying under the hot sun and letting it heal all the little bamboo nicks and all the cuts and sores festering from the damp, dirty jungle.

I daydreamed about making love to my lovely Dega beauty Ning. I wished that I could just lie in her arms and cry my eyes out, but my macho frame of mind in those days wouldn't allow that.

I started to think of those hopeless Americans' eyes below watching us depart, and I pushed that image from my mind. I thought about the next operation and figured it would be different. No idiot commanders would screw it up. No crooked counterparts would cut our legs from under us. No reporters would make us the bad guys again on the next operation, and the folks back home would love us as they used to. In those days when we were rough-and-tumble, innocent boys, staring in wide-eyed wonder at John Wayne in *Sands of Iwo Jima*. In those days, when John Kennedy said to us: *"Ask not what your country can do for you. Ask what you can do for your country."*

Maybe the next operation will be different, I thought. Maybe the next time we can really do our thing.

Thousands of feet below and behind me, an American Green Beret in a tiny cage stared at us flying away. He shrugged his battered shoulders, tears running down his cheeks. He wiped them away and smiled bravely. Maybe tomorrow they'll come and rescue me, but today I'm just going to survive for another day. It's kept me going so far, and I know my country will never desert me. I will never desert it.

I looked back and saw the Valley of the Plei Trap fade away in the distance. Damn, that rotor blast whipping through the chopper doors was wicked. It was making my eyes water like crazy. No matter how much I wiped them, they just wouldn't stop watering.

The Valley of Tears was, at last, behind me . . . but only for a couple of decades. That's not much more than a few months in the Orient. I pray to God I never let myself forget the Valley of Tears—and all it represents.

Montagnard Foundation, Inc.

Readers who would like to make a charitable contribution to the Montagnards may do so by sending their tax-free donations to the Montagnard Foundation, Inc., a South Carolina nonprofit corporation.

Make checks payable and send them to:

Montagnard Foundation, Inc.

PO Box 17064

Spartanburg, South Carolina 29301

All the monies collected are handled solely by Montagnards and are used totally for the benefit, education, and assistance of Montagnards both here and abroad.